Scriptures for the Church Seasons

Advent 2012

Preparing the Way

SUSAN MINK

An Advent Study Based on the Revised Common Lectionary

Abingdon Press / Nashville

PREPARING THE WAY
by Susan Mink

An Advent Study Based on the Revised Common Lectionary

Copyright © 2012 by Abingdon Press

ISBN-13: 9781426749636

Manufactured in the United States of America

12 13 14 15 16 17 18 19 20 21—10 9 8 7 6 5 4 3 2 1

Contents

Introduction

Waiting. That word has a bad connotation. We hate to wait. We think moments spent in lines, doctors' offices, and traffic are wasted time because we have so much to do, especially during this time of the year. We have presents to buy, decorations to put up, and plans to make. Who has time to wait? We are too busy preparing for Christmas.

When we imagine ourselves waiting, we are usually stuck in one place, not moving. But the dictionary also defines *waiting* as "looking forward expectantly" and "to be ready and available." Waiting does not have to be passive. We can wait productively, allowing God to prepare us for what is to come as we heed the call to "prepare the way" for God (Isaiah 40:3, New International Version[1]; Matthew 3:3). Preparing as we wait can be a deep and rewarding time as God grooms us for a deeper relationship and a deeper faith.

In Advent, we prepare the way for God as we wait for Jesus the Messiah. Messiah, or *mashiakh* in Hebrew, means "anointed one." In ancient Judah, kings were anointed during their coronation, so Messiah was the title for the legitimate king of Judah. After the Babylonian exile, the word "Messiah" came to mean something else to the Jewish people who were oppressed by foreign invaders. The Messiah became their vision of the one who could rule the Hebrew people according to God's ways once again. The Messiah would be the ideal king, ruling with justice and mercy while remaining faithful to the will of God. But when the Hebrew people returned to Jerusalem and installed a new king, it became clear that the new king was not the Messiah they had hoped for all those years. Subsequent kings turned from their faith and failed to rule with integrity. None of these rulers was God's Messiah.

The longing for the Messiah grew even stronger when Rome conquered the ancient Near East and ruled over Jerusalem. The Dead Sea Scrolls describe a warrior-king who would be sent by God and a king who functions as a high priest. This king would be from the royal line of King David and fulfill the words of 2 Samuel 7:12-13 where God promised David that one of his offspring would be on the throne forever. Today, we know this king as Jesus Christ.

Christ is the Greek word for "Messiah." Every time we say "Jesus Christ," we are affirming that Jesus is the anointed one. But Jesus redefined the messiah concept while he was on earth. Jesus was not the king of an earthly empire but of the kingdom of heaven. He did not come to overthrow political oppressors but the oppression of sin and death. Jesus instituted the new covenant, a fresh relationship with the Creator God. The Messiah introduced the beginning of a new world.

That world is still not here entirely. Jesus brought the kingdom of heaven to earth, but the world has yet to accept it. Like the sun breaking over the horizon, we anticipate its light while we still stand in the darkness. But we have unshakeable hope. Jesus promised his return, bringing the full glory of his worldwide rule as God's Messiah, the anointed one. Like the faithful in the centuries before us, we wait and prepare the way for the Messiah.

Thy Kingdom Come

Scriptures for Advent: The First Sunday
Jeremiah 33:14-16
1 Thessalonians 3:9-13
Luke 21:25-36

The word *Advent* is derived from a Latin word meaning "coming." Specifically, Advent means to prepare for the coming of Jesus Christ on earth. Advent studies usually focus on Jesus' birth, but why should we anticipate an event that happened over two thousand years ago? In today's busy world, we often think of Advent as a time for buying gifts, decorating our houses, and attending parties; in other words, we are preparing to celebrate a secular Christmas. Once the gifts are opened, the tree is down, and January slips in, we no longer think about Advent.

But we are living in a perpetual time of Advent here and now. Jesus Christ may have been born many centuries ago, but every season is one of anticipation for Christians. Jesus Christ has promised to return and bring a new reality that will be God's will "on earth, as it is in heaven."

Thinking about eschatology, the study of the end times, can be dis-turbing. Every few years or so, some-one announces a date for the end of the world, but we are still here. End-time preachers often threaten that everyone must "turn or burn." If we are comfortable in our lives, we do not want to think about everything ending. Eschatology gets relegated to the back burners of our faith, left to street preachers and religious fanatics.

However, eschatology is a key concept in our Christian beliefs. Threaded throughout Scripture in both the Old and New Testaments are promises that one day the world will live in harmony and jus-tice, and every being on earth will recognize the Lord as Creator and Ruler of the universe. From the vision of swords being beaten into plowshares in the Book of Isaiah to the promise of Christ returning on the clouds in Revelation, the Bible points us toward the future with anticipation and hope. We worship a God of restoration, and our faith calls us to prepare for Christ's return to heal the world. For Christians, every day is a day of Advent.

THE LORD IS OUR RIGHTEOUSNESS JEREMIAH 33:14-16

Hope can be dangerous. We have all heard the phrase "false hope," and we have recognized that hope can be cruel. Unrealistic hopes can blind us from reality. Hope is unsettling and can keep us in a state of indecision and uncertainty. We like for things to be certain, defined, and tied up neatly with a bow. Hope means that a situation is ongoing, and lack of closure can be as painful as a bad ending.

It would be hard to find a more difficult and messy situation than that of the prophet Jeremiah. He was God's prophet during the most unstable and tumultuous time in ancient Judah's history—the Babylonian invasions that occurred between 597–582 B.C., including the fall of Jerusalem to the Babylonians in 587 B.C. The city suffered a siege so horrific that people resorted to the cannibalization of children to survive (Jeremiah 19:9; Lamentations 4:10). Finally, the crippled city succumbed to the invaders who destroyed it once they entered. Jeremiah 33:10 describes the conquered city as "a wasteland, without humans or animals."

The king Zedekiah of Judah attempted to escape but was captured near Jericho. To ensure the end of his royal line, his sons were killed as he was forced to watch, and then his eyes were gouged out so the horrible scene of his sons' slaughter was the last sight he would ever see. He was brought in chains to Babylon to die as a prisoner (2 Kings 25:1-8).

Solomon's spectacular Temple, which housed the ark of the covenant, was burned to the ground. Everything in the Temple that was made of bronze, silver, or gold was plundered and carried off to Babylon. Seraiah, the chief priest, and Zephaniah, the second priest, were brought before the king of Babylon who put them to death (2 Kings 25:18-21).

The city of Jerusalem was shattered and so was the faith of the people. The Hebrew faith is built on covenants, or promises, God has made with them. The first is the promise of the land made to Abraham in Genesis 12–17 and reiterated to Moses in Deuteronomy 34:1-4. The land of Judah was intended for the Hebrew people, promised by God for centuries, but it was overrun and controlled by the Babylonians.

God also promised the Hebrew people a king descended from David. In 2 Samuel 7:16, God reveals his promise to David: "Your dynasty and your kingdom will be secured forever before me. Your throne will be established forever." A descendant of David on the throne was a concrete sign of God's promises to the Hebrew people. At the time, their king was blinded and imprisoned, and all his heirs were slaughtered on the plains of Jericho.

Most importantly, God promised to be the Hebrew people's protector and deliverer. God was their God, and they would be God's people. The Temple was a tangible sign of God in their midst. The innermost part of the Temple, the Holy of Holies, was only entered once a year by the high priest, who was consecrated for the moment when he stood before the ark of the covenant lest he be struck dead in God's holy presence. But after the invasions, the Temple was burned and ransacked, and the holy items of the Temple were plundered only for their value as precious metals. A foreign king slaughtered their priests. All the survivors of the invasion could see the smoldering wreckage of their beloved Temple on the highest hill of Jerusalem.

All of God's promises seemed to be shattered when the Babylonians conquered Jerusalem. Devastation was all around them. The burned-out streets were empty and cold. Jerusalem was no place for hope; in fact, the thought of hope was cruel, maybe even ridiculous. All indications were that the Hebrew people would be assimilated into Babylon, and their culture, history, and religion would become a brief historical footnote. It was at this exact moment of defeat when Jeremiah uttered the verses we read today. Despite the devastating real-

ity that was all around, Jeremiah promised restoration. God's promises were still viable. Even though the streets were strewn with corpses, Judah's princes lay slaughtered, and the Temple was smoking rubble, the people could trust in God's promises and feel hope.

Hope in God is never cruel or false. Hope is life-giving and life-affirming. It can be the force that keeps a person alive. Viktor E. Frankl, a World War II concentration camp survivor, wrote about this kind of hope in his book *Man's Search for Meaning*. Frankl wrote that the difference between a prisoner's survival and death was not his or her physical condition but his or her ability to see a future. Even for those in the camps, "there was an opportunity and a challenge. One could make a victory of those experiences turning life into an inner triumph, or one could ignore the challenge and simply vegetate, as did a majority of the prisoners."[1]

Jeremiah told his destroyed city that God would not only honor the covenants, but the future would be even better than the past. God would make a new covenant with them where God would engrave the law "on their hearts," and they would be the people of God (Jeremiah 31:33). Leading this new era would be a new king from the line of David who would restore Jerusalem and bring it to new heights of glory. Jerusalem would then become so aligned with the will of God that it will be renamed "The LORD Is Our Righteousness" (33:16).

Jeremiah 33:14-16 is very similar to Jeremiah 23:5-6 because both mention the new king who is named "The LORD Is Our Righteousness" (33:16). The new king and the new society share the name of righteousness. This new king will become the leader of God's new community. Not only will this new community live in safety and security, but it will also live according to God's rule. The New Jerusalem will demonstrate God's will on earth.

God's promises superseded the devastation and became a reality for the people of Judah. They were not assimilated as countless other peoples and cultures have been after decisive military defeats. They survived their exile and returned to rebuild Jerusalem, but from that day, they have waited for the righteous branch from David's line to come rule them. From that day, they have waited for the Messiah.

This hope has spread from this ancient band of Jewish exiles to shine throughout the world. We have met "The LORD Is Our Righteousness" in the person of Jesus Christ and have seen the church, his community on earth, struggle to live up to Jeremiah's vision of a community of righteousness. This is the hope that continues to illuminate a future for all of humanity and enables every follower of Christ to accept the challenge to turn every day into a victory.

How does the hope of the Messiah strengthen you in the midst of destruction? What does it mean to you to be waiting and preparing for "The LORD Is Our Righteousness"?

GLIMMERS OF THE KINGDOM
1 THESSALONIANS 3:9-13

What enables these communities of righteousness to survive? How has the church been able to continue in the midst of a world that has not yet realized God's will on earth? How does it offer glimmers of God's kingdom?

Thessalonica was the capital of Macedonia, now part of northern Greece. While it had a Jewish population, it was a melting pot of cultures and ethnicities with a subsequent variety of cults and religions. However, emperor worship flourished and was a crucial part of the social network of the city. The Thessalonians had built a statue of Augustus by the time Paul arrived in the city. The Christians would not participate in emperor worship. In a world where religion, business, and social position were interrelated, the Thessalonian church members fell outside of acceptable society. The members were ostracized and even seen as disloyal to the empire. No wonder the first churches were so tightly knit, and Paul was diligent in keeping contact with them.

Paul wrote this letter soon after Timothy had returned from Thessalonica. Paul had foreseen the pressures that the church would have and had discussed what they would have to suffer before he had left them. He was overjoyed to know that they had withstood so many difficulties, and the church was still faithful and courageous. Paul had prayed for them out of love and obedience. Paul knew that praying for others was not only the privilege but also the duty of the faithful. This duty is presented in 1 Samuel 12:23: "But me? I would never sin against the LORD by failing to pray for you." Paul did not just teach the Thessalonians about Jesus Christ; he consistently lifted them up to God in prayer, confident that his prayers would be heard and answered.

Paul's first letter to the Thessalonians is overflowing with love and encouragement. Paul repeatedly referred to the Thessalonians as his brothers and sisters and wrote of his strong desire to see them again. Even the thought of them brought Paul joy. These early Christians sometimes lost their family connections because of their faith, and the church was seen as a new family that would support and uphold one another. The cohesiveness of the church community strengthened the cohesiveness of their faith. Later in this letter, Paul addressed a primary concern of the Thessalonians that those who have died would miss the coming of Christ. Paul assured them that the dead would be lifted up to witness this incredi-

ble event with those who were still alive (4:13-14). Not even death can destroy the church community.

But no church is perfect, even if it is blessed and guided by God. In 1 Thessalonians 3:10, Paul prayed that God would make their faith complete or to "restore" (New Revised Standard Version[2]) or "supply" (NIV) whatever was lacking. Paul used the Greek word *katartizō*, which means to make something the way it should be or mend something, to describe the completeness of faith that he prayed for. Paul was praying that this Thessalonian church would be the embodiment of heaven on earth as expressed in the prayer Jesus taught to the disciples, "Thy kingdom come. Thy will be done in earth, as it is in heaven" (Matthew 6:10, King James Version[3]).

Even now, none of us is complete. We are living in a tension between what the world is now and what the world is meant to be. Jesus has given us a vision of the future where God's kingdom will come and all will live according to God's will, but we are still living in a world that does not live as it was created to live. War, bigotry, greed, selfishness, hatred, and apathy toward the suffering of others persist. People refuse to accept God as the Creator and King of the world and refuse to understand that God's Word is the blueprint for harmony within his creation. However, Paul reminded the Thessalonians of what is ahead: Christ will nians of what is ahead: Christ will come again, returning with all those who have devoted their lives to following him.

Imagine how wonderful the promise of Christ's return must have been to this small band of outcasts. Instead of existing on the edges of society, scorned and ignored, they would be included among the saints of God. This great event would be a reunion with Jesus Christ and all of Christ's followers. Those who lived as aliens and strangers in the world because of their faith would finally have a home.

Jeremiah promised a community of the righteous to the ancient Hebrew people. We are promised a time when perfect righteousness will rule the cosmos, and all will live within the justice and mercy of God. In that sense, we are living in the age of Advent as we await the final return of Jesus Christ.

In the meantime, the church's task is to show the world glimmers of heaven on earth. Every social institution reflects the larger society, but the church is called to exist within Jesus Christ. Therefore, the church exists and does God's work in the radical tension between our world today and the world of the future ruled by Jesus Christ. As a community that is devoted to the Word and the will of God, the church is to demonstrate love for one another, action for justice, and a dedication to mercy. Because we live in an imperfect world as imperfect peo-

ple, we do this imperfectly. The task seems impossible, but the resurrection of Jesus demonstrated that God is more powerful than sin and death. Christ's resurrection was a concrete example of the power of God that is and will be available to all Christians. Ephesians 1:18-20 includes this prayer:

I pray that the eyes of your heart will have enough light to see what is the hope of God's call, what is the richness of God's glorious inheritance among believers, and what is the overwhelming greatness of God's power that is working among us believers. This power is conferred by the energy of God's powerful strength. God's power was at work in Christ when God raised him from the dead and sat him at God's right side in the heavens.

This is the power that God has given the church through the Holy Spirit, and the power of all believers to create glimmers of God's kingdom on earth. We are called to a new life now, fueled by the power of Jesus Christ in our lives. We are also armed with the promise that God is not yet finished with creation, the church, and the world.

What does it mean to you to be part of God's driving force toward the future completion of God's kingdom? How do you see glimmers of God's kingdom on earth?

BE ALERT AND PREPARED
LUKE 21:25-36

The Apocalypse. It sounds terrifying, doesn't it? It has been the topic of disturbing paintings, haunting poetry, spine-tingling novels, and horror movies. But the word *apocalypse* means uncovering or revealing something that was previously unknown. Theologically, it is the story of God's ultimate triumph over evil. In other words, the Apocalypse is good news.

Matthew 24:4-36, Mark 13:5-37, and Luke 21:5-38 are similar and are collectively known as the Synoptic Apocalypse. The Apocalypse starts out sounding bad. There will be false prophets, wars, earthquakes, and famines. Jerusalem will be destroyed. Even the regular rhythms of the Earth will be disrupted. The paths of the stars, planets, the moon, and the tides will all become unpredictable. This is because the foundations of the cosmos will change. God will recreate by returning the world to chaos not seen since pre-creation and by rebuilding a new order.

This is not the first time God has disrupted the natural order but never before on this scale. A new star appeared in the sky on the night of Jesus' birth (Matthew 2:2). God split the sky and spoke down from the heavens when Jesus was baptized (Matthew 3:16-17; Luke 3:21-22). At the moment of Jesus' death on the cross, the Temple curtain tore and the earth shook (Matthew 27:51; Luke 23:44-46). But never before have the changes been as profound as they will be when Jesus Christ returns. The world will be recreated.

For centuries, the Jewish people had waited for the Messiah promised by Jeremiah. Prophets revealed more about his coming, but of all the prophecies, Daniel 7:13-14 was probably the best known among the Hebrew people. It reads:

As I continued to watch this night
vision of mine, I suddenly saw
  one like a human being
    coming with the heavenly clouds.
  He came to the ancient one
    and was presented before him.
  Rule, glory, and kingship
    were given to him;
    all peoples, nations, and languages
      will serve him.
  His rule is an everlasting one—
    it will never pass away!—
      his kingship is indestructible.

Revelation 1:7 echoes the vision in Daniel as it affirms Jesus Christ will come again and reign forever: "Look, he is coming with the clouds! Every eye will see him, including those who pierced him, and all the tribes of the earth will mourn because of him. This is so. Amen." Although the grand event will be earth-shattering and terrifying to those who do not understand, the faithful can raise their heads in hope and joy. Their persecutions are over. Since the cosmos will be ruled by the Word of

God and not by the desires of human beings, those who have been enslaved or oppressed will be redeemed to live as they were created to live.

This event is a sure thing. Just as a budding tree is a harbinger of spring, the cosmic upset Jesus described will usher in his return and establish God's kingdom on earth. Some commentators have suggested that the fig tree in Jesus' parable represents Israel, and the other trees represent all the other nations of the world. Others believe that Jesus was simply recasting a cosmic event into language his audience could understand. The important fact is the events have been set in motion, and Christ's return is inevitable.

When will these events happen? Luke 21:32 is problematic at first glance because the people whom Jesus was addressing have since passed away. But the Greek word for generation, *genea,* can also mean "era" or "age"; and any age may have particular characteristics such as waiting or suffering. While the time is unknown, a Christian's behavior in the meantime is clear. Believers are not to slip into a self-absorbed routine that puts faith on a back burner. Every day should be lived in the knowledge that the kingdom of God can and will appear either as glimmers of hope as faithful people attempt to live within the will of God, or as Christ creating a new world order.

Therefore, these promises are not just interesting theological footnotes but should inform our behavior and thoughts here and now. If we do not live and work in anticipation of Christ's return, the redemption offered by Jesus Christ is reduced from a world-saving cosmic event to merely an individual's personal salvation. While even one person's salvation is profound, dismissing Christ's return limits our understanding of Christ's work in the world today and in the future. If life were all about personal salvation, believers would only be interested in getting to heaven. Life becomes a narrow path focused on individual righteousness. The church could even become pockets of elitists who believe that they alone will be saved and the rest of the world will be damned. A church like this would believe that there is no need to be concerned with the rest of the planet because God is only interested in believers.

But Jesus tells us that the entire world is to be redeemed and transformed into a new reality where justice, mercy, and love rule in all circumstances. Because the church is aware of the hope and promise of Jesus' return, believers are called to participate in a future that Christ has already begun with his resurrection and victory over death. Believers are called to seek justice and mercy for others, actions that work to heal all the people of the world. Believers are called to love one another as Christ loves them, to abandon their own self-absorption, and to serve Christ without fear. These are not just exercises in religious obedience to get an individual to heaven but actions that build and strengthen God's kingdom on earth. Such actions offer ways to prepare for the fullness of God's kingdom that will rule the world one day.

Not long ago, I found an Advent hymnbook from 1849, compiled by James White from Oswego, New York. I expected to find lyrics from the hymns we sing at Christmas, but every hymn focused on Christ's return. For these people, celebrating Advent meant remembering how God had fulfilled the promise of the Messiah through the infant Jesus, and even more, looking forward to the promise of a healed and redeemed world. One of the hymns, "Lo! He Comes," can still be found in our hymnal:

> Lo, he comes, with clouds descending,
> Once for favored sinners slain;
> Thousand, thousand saints attending
> Swell the triumph of his train.
> Hallelujah! Hallelujah! Hallelujah!
> God appears on earth to reign.

> Yea, Amen! Let all adore thee,
> High on thy eternal throne;
> Savior, take the power and glory,
> Claim the kingdom for thine own.
> Hallelujah! Hallelujah! Hallelujah!
> Everlasting God, come down![4]

Why do you think such trepidation has surrounded Christ's second coming? Do you believe it is something to be anticipated or feared? In what ways can you prepare for God's coming kingdom?

---

[1] From *Man's Search for Meaning*, by Viktor E. Frankl (Simon and Schuster, 1959); page 93.
[2] New Revised Standard Version of the Bible, copyright 1989, Division of Christian Education of the National Council of the Churches of Christ in the United States of America. Used by permission. All rights reserved.
[3] Scripture quotations from The Authorized (King James) Version. Rights in the Authorized Version in the United Kingdom are vested in the Crown. Reproduced by permission of the Crown's patentee, Cambridge University Press.
[4] From *The United Methodist Hymnal* (Copyright © 1989 by The United Methodist Publishing House); 718.

Reflect the Messiah

Sometimes my husband jokes that he likes having people come over to our house because then he is sure we will clean it. Like our homes, our day-to-day lives can sometimes get sloppy if we do not anticipate scrutiny. Bad habits creep in. Good habits creep out. It is hard to be disciplined all the time.

As Christians, we are to live in a state of anticipation. God has promised a renewed and redeemed world through Jesus Christ, but God's work is still in progress. In the meantime, as redeemed people, the church is called to be the forerunner of the redeemed world. But it has been a while since we have heard those promises, and we are sloppy. Our relationship with God slips on our list of priorities. Soon, our spiritual homes are not fit for visitors at all.

Advent is meant to shake us out of our complacency. We clean and decorate our homes in anticipation of Christmas company. Advent is also a time to reevaluate our spiritual surroundings. How would we want Christ to find us when he comes back? What is missing in our lives? What is just unnecessary clutter? What means of spiritual housekeeping should we be doing as we look toward his arrival?

Discipline is not something most people enjoy, but it is the root of the word *disciple*. It is only through God's help that disciples find the discipline to live a life of righteousness. Yet, through God, this life of discipline becomes a life of freedom and of joy. It is a life of seeking God's kingdom and occasionally finding glimmers of God's glory breaking through on earth.

We prepare for the Kingdom to come by being part of the Kingdom right now. Since God has promised a world of justice, we anticipate the Kingdom by being just peacemakers. God has promised a world ruled by the righteousness of Jesus Christ, and we anticipate the Kingdom by mirroring Christ's righteousness in the world today. Living in obedience to Christ is not just an exercise in discipline. It is understanding and practicing what it means to celebrate Advent and being a part of the Kingdom on earth.

REFINING INTO RIGHTEOUSNESS
MALACHI 3:1-4

The Book of Malachi is the last book in the Hebrew Bible, the Old Testament. The most distinctive element of the book is the use of questions—twenty-two of them in fifty-five verses—to create the dynamic of an ongoing dialogue. The questions address the relationship between God and the people by asking how and why things were so. Clearly, there were serious difficulties in understanding God's covenant with the people in Malachi's time.

Malachi means "my messenger" in Hebrew, which may or may not have been the prophet's name. He probably lived about 450 years before Christ at a time when Judah was a minor province in the sprawling Persian Empire. The Temple had finally been rebuilt and rededicated about 50 years before Malachi after the Babylonians destroyed it in Jeremiah's time. The Jewish community at that time was probably small and relatively poor. The book is difficult to date because it is not concerned with specific events but an overall religious malaise of corruption, indifference, unfaithfulness, and lazy theological practices.

The people were not upholding their faith because they didn't believe that God was upholding the covenant. In Malachi 1:2, they asked, "How have you loved us?" intimating that they were not experiencing God's love. In Malachi 2:17, they asked the scathing question, "Where is the God of justice?" Things simply did not seem fair. Abusers and oppressors were prosperous while the faithful were struggling. It even seemed that God was pleased with those who ignored God's calls to live in justice and mercy. While they did not question God's existence, they did question what seemed to be God's lack of concern about their fate. God just did not seem to be involved in their lives.

God's response was to promise a dramatic reversal of reality. First, a messenger would warn them, and then God would come to the Temple. God would answer the cries for justice by purifying the Levites, the priests and keepers of the Temple. After the Temple was purified, God would judge those who oppress and abuse others (3:5). The spiritual and religious core would have to be refined before there would be justice in the rest of the nation.

The people of Malachi's time were people of the world just as we are. Verse five could describe today's world. It lists adulterers, perjurers, employers who cheat their employees, and those who take advantage of the weak and powerless. How could a world like this be purified in a way that would make it acceptable to God?

In those days, refining or purifying silver was a tedious process. While there are chemical methods of refining silver today, the ancient way, known as cupellation, is still one of the best ways to achieve very high purity. Silver is found in lead, so lead is the raw material. As the refiner heats the lead, a dark scum forms on top of the molten metal. If the temperature is kept high and precise enough for the proper amount of time, the lead oxidizes, the scum disappears, and the metal becomes bright as the silver is revealed. The refiner knows that the silver has achieved purity when he can see his reflection on the surface.[1]

Thus, after refinement, the people who were the spiritual core of the community would be a reflection of God's justice and mercy in the world. The people would know that this dramatic reversal would come soon after the arrival of the messenger mentioned in 3:1. Jewish tradition names Elijah as the messenger in this Scripture, and for centuries, the Jews have waited for Elijah's return to announce the coming of the Messiah.

Christians have found rich meaning in this passage from Malachi. Matthew 11:10, Mark 1:2, Luke 1:76, and Luke 7:27 all referenced Malachi 3:1 when they identified John the Baptist as the messenger who came to announce the imminent arrival of Jesus Christ. John the Baptist's task was to prepare the way for Jesus Christ by calling the people to be aware of their sins and repent. Then the Messiah would arrive and refine the spiritual core of society. From this core, God's justice and mercy would spread throughout the world. Thus, the question "Where is the God of justice?" would be answered. For Christians, the God of justice is found in Christ's followers.

This is exactly what we are told in Ephesians 4:32–5:1. Christians are called to be "be kind, compassionate, and forgiving to each other, in the same way God forgave you in Christ. Therefore, imitate God like dearly loved children." The people of God are to pattern themselves after God, empowered to do so by the work of Jesus Christ. Jesus as the refiner was sent to burn out the sins, or impurities, of God's people, enabling them to be a reflection of God in the world.

Jesus taught the people how it would be to live as God's reflection in the world. He clarified the Law, or Torah, which God had given to the people, demonstrating that it was not a list of rules and regulations but a way of life. Jesus taught that *Torah* means living in devotion to God not living in enslavement to dictates. By revealing the true meaning of God's commandments, Jesus brought the people's focus back to the maker of the law, God, rather than the Law itself. We cannot be a reflection of God without being in a deep relationship with God in the heart, mind, and soul.

Even more importantly, Jesus enabled the people to live this life of godly devotion. Silver cannot expel impurities by itself. It requires the careful attention of the refiner. In the same way, the people of God cannot become pure by their own effort. Through the agonizing path of the cross, Jesus burned through the domination of sin and death, refining the world so the kingdom of God could begin to grow. Malachi's image of "a refiner and a purifier of silver" (3:3) calls us today as it called the people of Judah and Jerusalem to offer ourselves again to God so that we might be purified like silver and reflect God's presence and power in our world.

During the week ahead, what actions can you take that would reflect God's presence in our world?

A DISCERNING FAITH
PHILIPPIANS 1:3-11

"I thank my God every time I remember you" (Philippians 1:13, NIV). What wonderful words to begin a letter! A friend of mine regularly writes "Phil 1:3" on the back of every envelope she sends to me and at the end of each email, and it never fails to make me feel loved and valued. When Paul wrote this to the Philippians, he was affirming their faith and their actions. Their faith would not wither away because of apathy or persecution. Paul was filled with joy thinking about this fledgling band of Christians, drawing strength and courage from them even as they looked to him as their leader and guide.

The Philippian church was centered in the Roman province of Philippi in Macedonia. Acts 16:16-40 tells about Paul's ministry in the city. In a dream, Paul was commanded to go to Macedonia. There, he drove a spirit from a slave girl and was beaten and thrown in prison. During the night, a miraculous earthquake flung open the prison doors, but instead of escaping, he and Silas stayed to convert the prison guards. He started a church in the home of Lydia, a merchant of purple cloth. Paul's converts were mostly, if not entirely, Gentile. They would have given up the emperor worship that was crucial to good social standing in a Roman city. At the time of this letter, the church was only ten years old. It had survived in a hostile environment and was strong enough to send Paul gifts of money to give to other struggling churches.

Paul wrote this letter while he was imprisoned, yet it is overflowing with joy. His love for this church is deeply personal, but it is more than a simple love between friends; it is a love that is enriched and intensified through their mutual love of Jesus Christ. The *Common English Bible* (CEB) translates Philippians 1:8 as "I feel affection for all of you with the compassion of Christ Jesus," but the original text reads, "with the very bowels of Christ." The bowels were thought to be the source of human emotion, as we would describe the heart today. Thus, Paul's love was not only inspired by Jesus but was also springing from Christ himself.

This church inspired Paul's confidence. God was clearly working in the lives of these people, and the good things they had accomplished were only a foreshadowing of things to come. Verse seven reads that Paul keeps the Philippians in his heart. The Greek word that is translated as "keep" suggests a deeper intensity than the English word. It has a cluster of meanings that include possession, clinging, and holding fast. Paul knew that they were with him in spirit while he was imprisoned, and they all were working to defend and support the gospel.

Paul continued with a prayer for the Philippians in verses 9-11. Read this prayer carefully because it says much about the foundation of faith. Paul's prayer says that we should seek to understand more about God, which leads to knowledge and insight. Knowledge and insight lead to discerning what is important in life. This discernment leads to living a life more in concert with Jesus. As we live closer to Jesus Christ, we also become closer to God and are able to see our fellow human beings through eyes of love. Living a life

of love is constant praise to God and to Jesus Christ because everyday actions reflect love that is centered in Christ. A life like this is a reflection of Jesus Christ in the world today.

He says a lot in a few verses. The prayer deserves closer examination. Paul prayed that the Philippians' love might grow to the point of overflowing but that the basis for this love is "knowledge and all kinds of insight" (verse 9). Paul wanted the Philippians to have an informed faith based on understanding and discernment. This discernment would show them the most important things in their lives.

What does discerning faith look like? Years ago, a friend gave me a necklace with Braille letters on it that read "blind faith." While I appreciated the thought, the words reflected poor theology, in my opinion. A living, growing faith is one that is constantly probing and searching for new understanding. While faith implies that we cannot understand everything, Paul prayed that the Philippians would not practice mere passive acceptance. Paul did not want them to simply believe what he told them but to discover the power of Jesus Christ in their lives for themselves. In fact, this passage is saying that without a constant search for knowledge and insight, we cannot discern how to live a life that is truly following Jesus Christ. Christians should never be afraid of searching and studying their beliefs. Exploring questions about faith helps to cull problematic thoughts and solidify beliefs that can withstand scrutiny. Galileo Galilei once said, "I do not feel obliged to believe that the same God who has endowed us with sense, reason, and intellect has intended us to forego their use."[2] Earnest questions and sincere exploration, partnered with prayer and careful discernment, only help to refine and purify our lives before Christ.

As we grow in insight and understanding, our love will also grow. Catching glimpses of God's nature helps us become more like God. We come to understand what God is doing in the world. Our wants become less important as we see the larger picture of God's plan. Since God is the source of love, then the "fruit of righteousness" mentioned in verse 11 is the ability to love both God and other people. This unselfish love is an embodiment of Christ. Lives of unselfish, Christ-like love are acts of praise. They are also glimmers of the kingdom of heaven that is to come.

This is what we were put on Earth to do. Twice in this passage, Paul mentions that Christ will one day return, which means the entire world will live within the love and fellowship of Christ. But while we can look forward in anticipation, the point of the Christian life is to open ourselves to let Christ do his wonderful work in us now.

It is so easy for life to distract us from the important things. Each morning, I make a list of things I would like to accomplish, but I suspect most people are just like me. I rarely cross everything off the list by the end of the day because I often lose focus on what I set out to do. I have spent my day distracted by things that seemed compelling at the time but were not meaningful in retrospect.

For Paul, the most meaningful thing was to concentrate on living life each day in such a way that the people of the church could be sincere and without shame on the day that Christ returns to earth. This was—and is—the focus of Christ's church on earth, then and today.

In what ways can you enrich or expand the capacity for a discerning faith in your life? How do you think the willingness to ask questions and gain new insights about God can increase your capacity to love?

COMING OUT OF THE WILDERNESS
LUKE 3:1-6

How many shopping days until Christmas? You probably hear it announced on the television and radio every day now. Stores advertise last-minute gifts, and websites publicize how many days are left to order with standard shipping. Everyone wants to remind you that there is not much time left, and there is a rush to prepare.

John the Baptist seemed to have the same sense of urgency. As a prophet of God, he heralded the beginning of Jesus' ministry on earth. John 1:6-8 states that John the Baptist was sent from God with a mission to "testify concerning the light." He was not the Messiah, but he came to herald his arrival, calling all who would listen into a state of readiness.

John the Baptist is a verified historical figure. The Book of Luke sets him into the social and political history of ancient Israel. Although it is not possible to pinpoint an exact date even with Luke's careful records, *The New Interpreter's Bible* places the beginning of John the Baptist's ministry somewhere around A.D. 28.[3] John the Baptist is mentioned in all four Gospels and in numerous other non-biblical sources, including the writings of the historian Josephus. John was the son of Zechariah, a priest "who belonged to the priestly division of Abijah" and served in the Temple. A descendent of Aaron, Elizabeth, John's mother, was also from a priestly family (Luke 1:5). Even though Elizabeth was past childbearing years, Zechariah had a vision that foretold John's miraculous birth. The Book of Luke tells us that Jesus and John the Baptist were relatives through their mothers. Commentators speculate that John was possibly under Nazarite vows because Luke 1:15 stipulated that he could not drink wine or liquor, and he practiced a restricted diet. Other historians suggest that he might have belonged to the Essenes, a group of ascetic desert-dwelling Jews who practiced immersion and associated water with God's Spirit.

Whatever he was, John the Baptist was a colorful character. He wore a coat made of camel hair with a leather belt like the prophet Elijah. He ate locusts and honey (Matthew 3:4). Although he was from the Aaronic line of temple priests, his ministry was in the desert just like the wilderness prophet Elijah. He baptized his followers in the Jordan River, which was long a symbol of new beginnings to the Jewish people because crossing the Jordan brought them into the Promised Land. Not only was the river significant, John chose to baptize at the very spot where Elijah was taken up into heaven (2 Kings 2:8). John's similarities to Elijah were not accidental. Since the time of Jeremiah, the Jewish people had been waiting for Elijah's return to announce the coming of the Messiah. The second to the last verse of the Old Testament, Malachi 4:5, reads, "Look, I am sending Elijah the prophet to you, before the great and terrifying day of the LORD arrives." Jesus identified John the Baptist as the fulfillment of the prophecy of Elijah in Matthew 17:10-13.

John lived in the desert wilderness. The land around Jerusalem is dangerous and inhospitable. The terrain is barren, rough, and rocky. When compared to orderly city streets and carefully tended gardens, it is unstructured and chaotic. Throughout Scripture, wilderness is the place of challenges and tests. The people of Israel were shaped into God's covenant people in the wilderness. David hid from King Saul in the desert caves of the wilderness. Jesus spent 40 days and nights in the wilderness being tested by Satan. It has long been a metaphor for a place of spiritual trials and transformations. As such, it has also been the symbol of a place of new beginnings. The wilderness returns people to a state where God can remold and recreate hearts and souls to something new. This is why John the Baptist's place was in the wilderness. He was not a minister of the established religious structure, but a prophet of transformation.

It makes sense that despite Luke's careful historical list of kings, governors, and priests, God's herald was an unknown prophet in the desert. John was calling for a new understanding of the way of God. John's baptism was one of *metanoia,* a Greek word most commonly translated as "repentance" in the New Testament. The CEB translates it as the baptism in which people showed that they were "changing their hearts and lives" (Luke 3:3). *Metanoia* is not merely being sorry for doing wrong. It is a complete reorientation of our lives to the direction and guidance of the Lord, dedicating ourselves to a deep and obedient relationship with God. It is a fresh, new way of understanding God's work in our lives and in society. Thus, John was preparing the people to be open to the new things that God was about to bring into the world through Jesus Christ, asking them to look to the power of God entering and changing humanity.

Luke 3:4-6 quotes Isaiah 40:3-5, which is a powerful vision of God's highway leading out of the wilderness. Think of this symbolism: Highways were primarily built for victory parades for kings in the ancient world, and God's arrival would be a joyous public event. When Isaiah quotes this Scripture, it suggests that the highway would lead from captivity in Babylon back to Jerusalem. In Luke, the symbolism is enlarged. Through Jesus Christ, this highway would be a way out of the wilderness, leading the way back home for all who were alienated, exiled, banished, or separated from God.

The construction of this road is a cosmic event. This path of righteousness changes the landmarks of the earth itself. Valleys are filled in and mountains are flattened. It creates a new way that was previously impossible. Luke ends the quote by writing, "All humanity will see God's salvation" (verse 6), which are words that are not in Isaiah. God's entrance into humanity is an earth-altering event, and every human being has the opportunity to be involved. The coming of the Messiah was not just for the Jews; it was for everyone.

In John's day, the earth was trembling at the brink of a new revelation—the Redeeming God made flesh and living amongst humans. John's tasks were to be aware of God's work in the world, point it out to people, ask them to realign themselves with God, and join in while holding out the vision of a redeemed society before them. Today, the world waits for Christ's return. In the meantime, the church's tasks are the same as John's tasks while waiting for God's redemption of the world. In other words, John is a role model for the church today.

What has been your experience with wilderness? How does John's call to repentance or to a change of hearts and lives speak to you?

---

[1] From *Knight's American Mechanical Dictionary*, by Edward Henry Knight (J.B. Ford and Company, 1872).
[2] From *How to Think About Weird Things*, by Theodore Schick, Jr. and Lewis Vaughn (McGraw Hill, 2002); page 112.
[3] From *The New Interpreter's Bible*, Vol. IX (Abingdon Press, 1995); page 80.

Prepare for Peace

***Scriptures for Advent:
The Third Sunday***
**Zephaniah 3:14-20
Philippians 4:4-7
Luke 3:7-18**

My niece is currently pregnant with her first child. At my last visit, she stroked her swelling tummy and smiled up at me. "I'm beginning to think of myself as a mother," she confided. As I looked around her apartment at all the preparations for the new baby, I told her that I was beginning to think of her as a mother too. She was transforming before my eyes. Her priorities had shifted. Her time, money, and energy were already being spent in different ways. Everything was centered on nurturing the new life within her.

During Advent, we look forward to and prepare for the entrance of a new baby in the world—Jesus Christ. We can look around our homes and see the preparations for his arrival. But are we beginning to think of ourselves as Christians? Have our priorities shifted to welcome Jesus Christ into our lives? How are we spending our time, energy, and money? How effectively are we nurturing the new life within us?

At the moment that Jesus Christ enters our lives, what was once standard and acceptable behavior needs to be reexamined. Instead of measuring ourselves by society's guidelines, we strive to meet God's guidelines. However, preparations for the birth of Jesus Christ in our lives go beyond behavior. Just as a new mother changes her self-identity when she first holds her newborn, we are asked to change our self-identity when Jesus Christ enters our lives. We do not just act like different people; we *are* different people. Our lives become infused by what the apostle Paul referred to as "the fruit of the Spirit," which he names as "love, joy, peace, patience, kindness, goodness, faithfulness, gentleness, and self-control" (Galatians 5:22-23). Preparing for the coming of Jesus means that we allow ourselves to be refined and remolded into followers of Jesus.

In the same way I saw the change in my niece, others will see the change as we prepare for the coming of Jesus into our lives. God's work in people is reflected outwards. Christ becomes visible through the people who have allowed him to work a transformation in their lives.

During pregnancy, a family prepares the way for a precious new life that will transform them forever. Advent is the time for us to evaluate how well we welcome Jesus Christ into our lives and how his arrival has transformed our lives forever.

CALMED WITH LOVE
ZEPHANIAH 3:14-20

How long did it take you to find the Book of Zephaniah? It is one of the more obscure books in the Bible. Zephaniah is the ninth of the twelve books of prophets at the end of the Old Testament. Historians and biblical scholars know little about the man Zephaniah, but he is referred to as "Zephaniah, Cushi's son" (Zephaniah ben Cushi) in Zephaniah 1:1 , which gives a small clue to his background. *Cushi* means "African" in Hebrew, and *ben* means "son of." His knowledge of Jerusalem and the Temple and his compassion for the people suggest that he was from Jerusalem. His genealogy in Zephaniah 1:1 is unusually long and ends with the name Hezekiah, which leads historians to question whether he was of royal blood, descended from King Hezekiah.

Historians place his ministry somewhere between 630 and 620 B.C., during the beginning of the reign of King Josiah. At that time, the Temple was housing pagan priests and prostitutes. God was still being worshipped, but the worship was in tandem with worship of other deities.

The Book of Zephaniah begins with a description of vast destruction. God narrates a horrific scene of sweeping away animals, birds, fish, and people. What God creates, God is also able to destroy. The Book of Zephaniah seethes with God's righteous anger against those who turned away from God's law.

King Josiah rediscovered God's Book of Law, and 2 Kings 23 details his reforms. In the 18th year of Josiah's reign, a book of God's law—probably an early version of Deuteronomy—was discovered in the Temple. After reading it, Josiah commanded that it be read before all the people of Judah. He then made a public covenant with God "that he would follow the LORD by keeping his commandments, his laws, and his regulations with all his heart and all his being in order to fulfill the words of this covenant that were written in this scroll" (2 Kings 23:3). King Josiah made good on his promise. He removed all the pagan items from the Temple and burned them. He tore down outlying shrines and places of human sacrifice. He deposed the pagan priests and defiled all the sites of pagan worship. After the land had been made pure again, King Josiah commanded the people to celebrate Passover, which had not been celebrated for many years.

Zephaniah 3:9 marks a dramatic turning point in the Book of Zephaniah. The book is a chilling description of God's wrath and destruction until that verse. But from that verse until the end of the book, God is tender and loving toward his people instead of acting as the terrifying destroyer. The book ends with a joyous celebration, perhaps mirroring Jerusalem's celebration of Passover. The relationship between the world and God had been radically altered.

What had changed? Zephaniah 3:9-13 quotes God, telling the people that he will purify them. Instead of remaining headstrong, haughty people, they will serve God "as one" (verse 9). They will be humble and seek refuge in God (verse 12). Verse 17 joyfully proclaims that God is in their midst. God has come into the city to heal the people. The description of God's love and care is as powerful and compelling as the previous description of destruction. God promises to remove all reason to fear. He will "change their shame into praise" (verse 19). He promises to gather up the lost and frightened and bring them home. Mercy does not make him weak. Instead, this great warrior is "mighty to save" (verse 17, NIV). Not only do the people rejoice over God, but God also rejoices over the people. God himself breaks into exultant singing (verse 17).

What an amazing vision of God! When is the last time your heart has been so full of joy that you broke out in song? Our Lord is not reserved and solemn. God is described here as overflowing with delight, lavishing love and care on his people. These are the same people who had turned their backs on God; however, like the father in the parable of the Prodigal Son who rushes out with gifts as soon as his son approaches (Luke 15:11-32), God brushes aside their shame and showers them with love and restoration. God fashioned creation to be in relationship with him and rejoices with abandon when relationships are restored.

In the midst of all this joy, there is a phrase in Zephaniah 3:17 that is translated in several ways. The NIV translates this phrase as "he will quiet you with his love." The NRSV translates it as "he will renew you in his love." The KJV interpretation is "he will rest in his love." The CEB states that God "will create calm with his love." All these translations suggest a rich feeling of calm, peace, and renewal given through God's love. Perhaps this is what Zephaniah meant. Certainly the people needed calming. They had forgotten their Creator and Lord to the point of losing his Law in the Temple. They understood the depth of their sin. From 3:12 until the end of the book, there is no mention of the terrible betrayals and transgressions the people have committed. God has forgiven and forgotten their sins and is silent about them. Despite their terrible actions, these people do not need to be anxious in the presence of God. Their fears are quieted. Through God's love, they have become confident and renewed. The restoration of relationship is complete.

Being human can be messy. Betrayal and sin come easily to human hearts, yet God comes into our midst to heal the brokenness. All who realize their sin, turn their backs on betrayal, and dedicate themselves to living in covenant with God give cause for God to sing with joy. The song is one of miraculous forgiveness. It is a song of healing and renewal, of gathering up and bringing home. It is a song of the peace of God.

How do you feel about the idea that God sings with joy over you? In what ways has God calmed you with his love?

DON'T WORRY
PHILIPPIANS 4:4-7

"Don't worry." That is a command most of us would say is doomed to failure. Humans often dwell on the negative, weaving all sorts of horrific scenarios of failure and embroidering events with dark, ulterior motives. Anxiety has become a national epidemic. According to Alice Park in an article for *TIME* magazine, about 18 percent of the US population has a diagnosed anxiety disorder.[1] When we read Paul's words to the Philippians telling them not to worry about anything, we may think his instruction sounds impossible. Paul's situation, however, was anything but easy.

If anyone had things to worry about, it was Paul. His fledgling churches were bombarded with false theologies and pagan ideas. They were plagued with infighting and confusion about their beliefs. In many cases, they were socially ostracized and even persecuted. Paul had been criticized for teaching false theology. He had been beaten, imprisoned, and run out of town on numerous occasions. He had a physical ailment that was a "thorn in [his] body" (2 Corinthians 12:7-10). At the time he wrote this letter to the Philippians, he was in prison (Philippians 1:7, 12-18). In fact, every area of his life seemed to be a worthy subject for anxiety.

Paul had found the peace of God. This was not a sunshine-and-rainbows kind of optimism that refused to acknowledge real problems. His letters deal with specific difficulties and issues, both personal and within the churches. He was rational and realistic about the challenges ahead. Through all of his difficulties, Paul relied on God.

How did he do that? He gave the Philippians clear instructions. First, he told them to rejoice in the Lord. In order to be joyful about something, we must be aware of it and think about it. Therefore, Paul was telling them to keep God foremost in their minds. Next, he told them, "Let your gentleness show in your treatment of all people" (Philippians 4:5). The Greek word *epieikēs* is translated as "gentle," and the Greek word has a rich meaning. It suggests that which is equitable, fair, and mild, qualities indicative of a consideration for others and a lack of selfishness. It is wisdom and grace in dealing with other people, qualities that were demonstrated by Jesus Christ.

A Native American proverb tells about a grandfather who told his grandson about two wolves who were constantly battling inside his heart. One wolf was greed, hatred, and fear. The other was love, peace, and kindness. "Which will win?" asked the grandson. The grandfather replied, "The one I feed."[2]

Indulging in irritability with others is self-centered and self-destructive. Paul was instructing the Philippians to "feed the good wolf" so that they would reflect the love of Christ to others. Living within the will and inspiration of Christ would bring him near, strengthening their relationship with him even further.

Paul's counter to worry was prayer. Prayer is not a last resort of the panic-stricken. It is turning problems over to God, waiting for direction, and accepting that God is in control. Prayer is also recognizing that if God is in control, we are not. Devout prayer is a deep demonstration of trust in God. Trust in God means that God will be with us, support us, and guide our pathways in directions that are ultimately good, even if it is not what we would choose. Therefore, worrying is mistrusting the character and nature of God. The history of faith and Scripture tell us that God loves humanity deeply and is involved with each person's life. Each time we experience God, we see glimpses of the character of God. How comforting it is to know that God is always the same loving, compassionate, and wise God! By presenting everything to God in prayer, our struggles are now before the most powerful being in the cosmos, the One who loves us dearly.

This does not mean that bad things cannot happen. Tradition tells us that Paul was martyred in Rome. God continues to work in a sinful world filled with pain and brokenness. Yet by turning our worries over to God, we experience the peace that comes from trusting God's love, power, and guidance. When we pray, we do not passively wait for God to fix everything; we open ourselves to God's direction and respond by working with God in the world in accordance with our faith.

Paul wanted the Philippians to "adopt the attitude that was in Christ Jesus" (2:5). In John's Gospel, Jesus explained this concept to the disciples by using the metaphor of the vine and the branches; he was a vine, and they were the branches (15:1-5). While the vine can survive without the

the branches, the branches cannot survive and flourish without the vine. They draw nourishment from the vine, depend on the vine for support, and ultimately grow to look like the vine. Abiding in Christ means that you live in unity with Christ, in obedience to Christ, and as a reflection of Christ. When we abide with Christ, we understand the peace of God, a serenity that transcends all circumstances. Oswald Chambers, in his classic devotional *My Utmost for His Highest,* wrote, "God's mark of approval, whenever you obey Him, is peace. He sends an immeasurable, deep peace; not a natural peace, 'as the world gives,' but the peace of Jesus."[3] Paul communicates this same sense of peace in his instructions to the church at Philippi.

In Philippians 4:7, the Greek word *eirēnē* is translated as "peace." The word suggests far more than just the absence of conflict; it includes such qualities as harmony, concord, security, safety, prosperity, and felicity. When Paul talked about peace, he was describing the results of restored relationships among human beings and between human beings and God. For Christians, peace means a wholeness of being and an inner serenity that comes from the love of God and the salvation of Jesus Christ. Jesus offered this kind of peace in John 14:27 when he told his disciples, "Peace I leave with you. My peace I give you. I give to you not as the world gives. Don't be troubled or afraid."

When a person is full of the peace of God, worry dissipates. Rejoicing becomes second nature. Humanity was created for this state of existence. This is the marvelous gift that God presents to followers of Jesus Christ. This is the peace on earth that made the angels sing.

What do you worry about? How can the peace of God help you in those situations?

WHAT, THEN, SHOULD WE DO? LUKE 3:7-18

What defines someone as a Christian? A Christian is defined as "a person who believes in Jesus Christ."[4] As Christmas approaches, many people who don't think about Jesus most of the year will prepare to celebrate. Churches get ready for the once-a-year crowds that attend their annual pageants and Christmas Eve candlelight services. It seems more people call themselves Christians during Advent than during the rest of the year.

For John the Baptist, the question was about much more than how people identified themselves. It was also about how they lived. Being a person of faith was not about what you said or called yourself, but about your commitment to God, a commitment demonstrated by your actions.

John's approach to ministry would no doubt make evangelism committees shudder. His teachings

PREPARING THE WAY

were compelling enough to make crowds of people trek across the desert to the Jordan River to be baptized. But instead of warmly welcoming them and praising them for their effort, he challenged them, calling them snakes and questioning their right to be there. Can you imagine the same welcome as the crowds line up at churches this Christmas Eve? John the Baptist's approach was a full-scale assault on religious complacency.

In Matthew 3:7, John's fiery remarks are addressed to some Pharisees and Sadducees who had come to be baptized. In Luke's version, John addresses the crowd. Although the crowds had made the trip to the desert to be baptized, John questioned their motives. "Who warned you to escape from the angry judgment that is coming soon?" he taunts. According to John, the people standing in front of him were the ones who deserved God's judgment. If they thought that their background and lineage as ancestors of Abraham would be enough to shield them from judgment, John tore down their sense of security. Racial or religious heritage has no weight when it comes to salvation. It did not matter that they had been raised in the faith. God could create people with those same credentials from the stones on the ground!

John's words should send a chill through all who feel secure practicing an easy, undemanding faith. We cannot claim salvation with unchanged lives. Dietrich Bonhoeffer, a German theologian and martyr, called such complacent religion "cheap grace." He wrote, "Cheap grace is the grace we bestow on ourselves. Cheap grace is the preaching of forgiveness without requiring repentance, baptism without church discipline, Communion without confession.... Cheap grace is grace without discipleship, grace without the cross, grace without Jesus Christ, living and incarnate."[5] Cheap grace is going through the motions of faith without showing any evidence of a true relationship with God.

If complacent faith is cheap grace, what is a life of costly grace? What does repentance look like? John's answer focused on social justice. In ancient Israel, wearing sackcloth, a rough fabric, and ashes on the forehead demonstrated repentance. Here, John's instructions are less dramatic and more pragmatic. Those who have more than they need should give to those who are needy. Someone with two tunics should give one to someone with none, and someone with extra food should feed the hungry. Tax collectors, notorious for defrauding citizens, were to be honest in their dealings. Soldiers were not to threaten or extort people (Luke 3:10-14). Greed and exploitation are indicators of false repentance and an unchanged life. Noticing others in need and responding in genuine concern is a glimmer of God's kingdom in the world.

Understandably, the crowds began to wonder if John the Baptist was the Messiah. John denied it, saying that he was not worthy to untie the Messiah's sandals, a duty reserved for menial slaves (verse 16). The Messiah would be much more powerful than he. As an illustration, he compared the baptisms he was administering with those of the Messiah. John's baptism was with water and symbolized cleansing, repentance, and renewed allegiance and submission to God's will (see Isaiah 1:16-17; Ezekiel 36:25-26). In contrast, the Messiah would baptize "with the Holy Spirit and fire" (Luke 3:16). Various interpretations of this baptism suggest the purifying work, power, and judgment of God's Spirit. The images are echoed in the account of the Pentecost in Acts 2.

In the ancient times, after wheat was harvested, farmers would toss the grain into the air with a winnowing fork. The wind would catch the light outer hull, or chaff, and blow it away, while the good grain would fall to the ground. John used this illustration, saying that the Messiah would destroy the chaff while gathering up and saving the wheat. The valuable kernel would be all that was left.

It is human nature to identify with the good or the evil, the wheat or the chaff. However, when grain is harvested, every kernel has an outer hull. Each piece is made up of both something valuable and something worthless. In every one of us, there is chaff that needs to be burned away, chaff that prevents us from experiencing the peace that comes from a close relationship with God through Jesus Christ.

John's harsh words resonate in our lives as we prepare ourselves for the coming of Jesus Christ. When Christ enters lives, the light of God illuminates our need for renewal. The baptism of fire and the Holy Spirit burns through our hearts, cleansing us of what keeps us from a close relationship with God. We are empowered to live according to God's will. We are empowered with the full knowledge of God's never-ending, all-encompassing love. God's power in Jesus Christ moves us to change our lives and gives us peace.

How do your actions reflect your faith in God? What chaff in your life needs to be burned away so you can experience God's peace?

---

[1] From "The Two Faces of Anxiety" by Alice Park, *TIME Magazine* (December 5, 2011); page 56.
[2] From *http://thinkexist.com/quotes/native_american_proverb/*.
[3] From *My Utmost for His Highest*, by Oswald Chambers (Discovery House Publishers, 1935); quote from devotion dated December 14.
[4] See www.dictionary.com *http://dictionary.reference.com/browse/Christian.*
[5] From *The Cost of Discipleship*, by Dietrich Bonhoeffer (Simon & Schuster, 1959); pages 44-45.

Images of the Messiah

Scriptures for Advent:
The Fourth Sunday
Micah 5:2-5a
Hebrews 10:5-10
Luke 1:39-45

What is your image of Jesus? Many of us would think of the well-known painting "Head of Christ" by Warner Sallman, which has been reproduced more than 500 million times since it was painted in 1941, according to its publishers.[1] Others might think of a portrayal of Jesus in movies they have seen or a print that hung in their Sunday school classroom. This time of year, we might imagine a baby in a manger. Most images of Jesus I recall from childhood are of a gentle, white-robed man surrounded by sheep or small children. Although those images are in Scripture, the Jesus portrayed throughout the Bible isn't simple or easy to understand. Because of his nature—man yet God—the images of Jesus in the Bible are complex and complicated, some familiar, some strange, some approachable, and some puzzling.

In ancient times, the people looked to the future for their Messiah. Would he be a powerful warrior who would destroy their enemies so that they could finally live in peace? Would he be a king who would rule over the land with justice, ending social oppression? Would he bring prosperity and end hunger and poverty? Would he be able to gather up and bring home all the people who had scattered during foreign invasions? When Jesus arrived, it didn't seem to get any easier to define him. Was he a political rebel bent on overthrowing Rome? a religious zealot who would destroy the ancient temple system? a miraculous healer? a common criminal? Or was he really the Son of God?

The passages that follow describe Jesus in different ways. The first passage is an Old Testament image written about 700 years before Jesus' birth. Images of the Messiah and God-inspired prophecy intertwine to speak to the hopes of the people. Next is an epistle probably written in the 60's or 80's A.D.[2] that explains Jesus' role as the sacrificial high priest. Last is the heartfelt cry of the first person to recognize and claim the unborn child in Mary's womb as her Lord. Each image offers a view of the complex, confusing, and thrilling person of Jesus Christ.

THE SHEPHERD
MICAH 5:2-5a

The Book of Micah has long been a challenge for biblical scholars and commentators. The core of the book is attributed to a prophet named Micah, a shortened form of *Micaiah,* whose name means "Who is like Yahweh?" He probably lived around 700 B.C., roughly the same time as the prophet Isaiah. However, most scholars agree that other unnamed prophets have added to Micah's original writings, contributing later inspirations and insights.

The book describes a cycle of the wrath of God and God's forgiveness and mercy. These cycles could have been tied to the invasions of the Assyrians or the Babylonians. Thus, biblical scholars have speculated that Micah 5:2-5a was written for those who were in exile and waiting to return home. These displaced people hoped for a king from the line of David on the throne in Jerusalem to rule them, but that never happened. The city was rebuilt. The Temple was restored. But a descendent of King David never sat on Jerusalem's throne again.

Perhaps the prophecy speaks of a different kind of king. In fact, this passage does not use the Hebrew word for king, *melek,* but instead uses the word *mashal,* which means someone who rules or has dominion. Perhaps Micah used the word *mashal* because this would not be a king in the conventional sense. This would be a different kind of king.

Verse 2 tells us that this ruler would come from the humble, undistinguished little village of Bethlehem, King David's hometown. Situated about six miles south of Jerusalem, Bethlehem was first mentioned in Genesis 35:19 as the burial place of Rachel, the wife of Jacob. In line with God's habit of making something great out of something that seems inconsequential by human standards, this town that would be home to the greatest ruler of the planet was so small and nondescript that it was almost an afterthought in the clans of Israel. In *The Message,* Eugene Peterson refers to Bethlehem as "the runt of the litter" (Micah 5:2).[3]

This ruler would also have deep roots in Israel's history. Those who listened to verse 2 in Micah's time would have immediately thought of the Davidic covenant, forged by God in 2 Samuel 7 and 1 Kings 2:4. The Davidic covenant promises eternal kingship for a descendent of David. Thus, verse 2 would be interpreted to mean that Micah's king would be a blood descendent of King David.

Most importantly, this ruler would be someone who would govern for God. He would find the strength and authority to rule through the power of God. Rather than the long line of kings before him who abandoned the ways of God, he would remain steadfast in the faith. The people, Israel and the entire world, would live in peace and security under his dominion.

No wonder this passage has been used for centuries during Advent. For Christians, this king could be none other than Jesus Christ. In fact, this passage was referenced in Matthew's story of the birth of Jesus. After the wise men, or magi, asked King Herod where the newborn king of the Jews could be found, he gathered his priests and scribes to find the answer. They replied that the prophets had written the following:

You, Bethlehem, land of Judah,
　by no means are you least
　among the rulers of Judah,
　because from you will come
　one who governs,
who will shepherd my people Israel
　(Matthew 2:6).

Micah 5:2-5a gave hope and comfort to the people of Micah's time; later Christians understood the passage as a glimpse forward to the future when Jesus Christ would reign as God's anointed ruler.

What kind of ruler does this passage describe? Verse 4 portrays him as a shepherd, a common attribute associated with David and his descendants. David was a boy-shepherd who became Israel's greatest king. The metaphor is also used to describe God in Psalm 23; Ezekiel 34; and Micah 2:12; 4:6-8. In John 10:1-18, Jesus described himself as the good shepherd. Shepherding was usually a job for the youngest, least important son or a hireling. It was a low-class, low-status position. Shepherds lived with their sheep in field conditions, sleeping near them and keeping them safe. Shepherds could recognize each one of their sheep and knew them by name. They carried them when they were injured. Their lives revolved around the needs of their sheep. The shepherd metaphor works well as a description of an ideal ruler.

Micah 5:3 is a bit of a puzzle. Is it a reference to the real pain that was and still is in the world while we wait for a Messiah to come? Does it refer to the mother of a king to come? At the time this Scripture was written, the people of Israel were scattered because many of them were exiles or refugees in foreign lands. Today, many people are scattered, living as refugees and exiles in mental and emotional places that take them far from God and from one another. This promised ruler will remove barriers that keep people apart from one another and reconcile scattered families (verse 3). It is easy to understand why Christians find such meaning in Micah's words and apply his words to the stories of the birth of Jesus.

But most of all, this ruler is a king of peace. His peace is not the comfort of an elite group of people but a worldwide, all-encompassing peace. A peace like this can only exist and be maintained by compassionate justice. Such peace has the potential to heal the entire world.

Back in the days of Micah, God gave the prophets hope by revealing glimpses of the future with a ruler who would reestablish God's justice, mercy, and peace. The pain of the present would ultimately yield joy and new life. The people would be able to live with a sense of security (verse 4).

Today we live in the tension between God's kingdom that has begun here on earth and the continuing promise of a fully healed and reconciled world. Christians find sustenance in the words of Micah. We see these promises fulfilled in the birth of Jesus Christ, and we look forward to the full establishment of God's realm of mercy, justice, and peace in the second coming of Jesus Christ. Our challenge is to be subject to the rule of Christ in our lives here and now while we wait for the entire world to live within his power.

When you experience tough times, what hope do you find in the words of Micah? What does the image of the shepherd say to you about God's care?

THE SACRIFICIAL PRIEST
HEBREWS 10:5-10

Micah's Scripture describes the Messiah by using the image of a shepherd king. The letter to the Hebrews talks about Jesus as a high priest. Both images reveal power and authority, but they also reveal humility and service. We see in these images important aspects of the character of Jesus Christ, who became one of us in order to heal the broken, scattered, and fearful.

The image of the high priest is presented initially in Hebrews 2:17 and is developed throughout the letter. Hebrews 10:5-10 elaborates upon the image of the human Jesus as a high priest who offers himself as a sacrifice once and for all. Fred B. Craddock calls the image of Jesus as high priest "the extraordinary theological achievement at the heart of the letter." According to Craddock, "Being one of us not only qualified Jesus to be a merciful priest but also equipped him to be the model to whom believers look."[4] He points to this idea as it is expressed in 12:1-3, which refers to Jesus as the "pioneer and perfecter" of our faith.

Who was the high priest and how did the high priest function in the ancient temple rituals? The high priest was a descendent of Aaron who was the head of all the altar priests and who performed the rituals for the Day of Atonement. Leviticus 16 details the instructions for these rituals (see also Leviticus 4:1–5:13; 23; Numbers 28–29). It was celebrated on the tenth day of the seventh month with a series of rituals meant to purify the sanctuary and the people. The purification was considered necessary in order to restore them as agents of God's presence in our world.

Before the Temple in Jerusalem was destroyed, the people believed that throughout the year, the sins of the people would collect in the Temple, defiling it. It was therefore crucial to cleanse the Temple so that it would remain an acceptable dwelling place for God. The high priest would take the blood of a bull, sacrificed for his personal sins, and the blood of a goat, sacrificed specifically to cleanse the Temple, and sprinkle the blood on the mercy seat, the cover of the ark of the covenant. It was considered the "detergent" that would cleanse the Temple of sins, although the cleansing was temporary and had to be done again the next year. The need for purification indicates the understanding that sin had the power to infect both people and institutions. The rituals also reflect the understanding that God does not abandon a repentant sinner.

Hebrews 10:5-10 contrasts the role of Jesus as high priest against the ancient understanding of high priests and the ritual practice of sacrifice. Every year, purification had to be repeated. Every year, people had to face their sins and repent in order to be worthy before God. Every year, people came before God to be purified of the sin and guilt that separated them from God. Hebrews 10:3-4 reads, "Instead, these sacrifices are a reminder of sin every year, because it's impossible for the blood of bulls and goats to take away sins."

According to the writer of Hebrews, the system is flawed. Psalm 40:6-8, rephrased in Hebrews 10:5-7, says that what God really wants is not empty ritual but people who do God's will and have God's law within them. These words echo the ancient prophetic warnings against excessive dependence on ritual and their call to obey God's will and observe God's law within the heart (See also 1 Samuel 15:22; Psalm 50:8-10; Isaiah 1:10-13; Jeremiah 7:21-24; Hosea 6:6; Amos 5:21-26). Without sincere dedication and obedience, animal sacrifices and temple cleansings are empty rituals. What was needed was not more ceremonial cleansing by animal blood, but a way to break the cycle of sin and guilt. What was needed was a new relationship between God and humanity.

Hebrews 10:7 interprets Psalm 40:6-8 with the voice of Jesus who says, "Look, I've come to do your will, God." The text in Hebrews changed a line that read "but you have given me ears!" (Psalm 40:6), meaning that God gave the psalmist the will to listen to God's direction, to "but you prepared a body for me" (Hebrews 10:5).

Jesus became human to reforge the covenant between God and humanity. By taking the place of the ineffective animal sacrifice, Jesus changed the entire dynamic. The offering of Jesus Christ ended the need for any other sacrifice. It forever cleared the way for humanity to stand without shame before God. The writer of Hebrews presents this change with Jesus in the role of the sacrificial high priest. This high priest offers himself as a perfect and eternal sacrifice. He gives himself for others.

In ancient days, the high priest was the mediator between God and the people. It was only the high priest who was permitted to enter the innermost sanctum of the Temple, the Holy of Holies, where the ark of the covenant was placed. Jesus took over the role of the high priest and offered himself as the final, ultimate sacrifice (Hebrews 7:26-27).

And so everything is new. The difference goes beyond getting out of a yearly ritual; it is a fresh, new relationship, a new covenant. As human beings, we still sin, but our interaction with God's grace and presence is no longer tied to sacrifice. Through Christ's incarnation, the cycle of sin and forgiveness is broken, and we can move beyond that to establish a meaningful relationship with an intimate, loving God. The tension between the almighty Creator God and sinful humanity is over. Through Christ, we are forgiven, now and forever. What an incredible act of love!

It is important to know that the point of tension was not God's love for humanity. God never sought to withhold love. But sin keeps us out of a full relationship with God, like a disobedient child who hides fearfully in the closet when his or her parent comes home. Jesus' sacrifice communicated to us, *Whatever it is that you've done, it's covered. There is no reason to fear. You cannot destroy my love.*

We still have to deal with the effects of sin. The world is still not entirely within God's will, and we do things that are counter to God's plan for the world. Sin damages the fabric of creation and hurts all of humanity. Atonement does not mean that we can live free of consequences. Christ's sacrifice does not make repentance obsolete because repentance means recognizing sin and turning away from it to a new life in God's will. Atonement does mean that God is always and forever in relationship with us, and even the power of sin cannot destroy that. Jesus' sacrifice means that we do not have to worry about our sins damaging God's love for us. Because we are forgiven forever, we can be bold and confident in our relationship with the Holy God.

As high priest and mediator, Jesus Christ stands on the altar of sacrifice, reaching out to join us forever with God. Hebrews teaches that because of his willing self-sacrifice, we are worthy to be in the presence of Almighty God. In addition, we can look to Jesus as an example of our capacity to live obediently with God's law in our own hearts.

What does living according to God's will mean to you in your life of faith? What does the image of Jesus as the high priest who offers himself as the ultimate sacrifice suggest to you about giving yourself to others?

A CHILD IN THE WOMB
LUKE 1:39-45

Have you ever thought what it must have been like for Mary? She was a young, unmarried girl with an unbelievable story to explain her pregnancy. Explanations given by an angel probably did not help her situation. Although Scripture does not address her difficulties, we can just imagine the reaction of her parents and the townspeople. We know that Joseph nearly cancelled the wedding when he found out she was pregnant. In fact, Deuteronomy 22:23-24 stipulates that a betrothed virgin, along with her lover, should be stoned if she laid with a man before the wedding. Perhaps that is why Mary travelled to visit Elizabeth. It might have been easier to be far away from watchful eyes and gossiping tongues.

Elizabeth would understand. She was pregnant herself, and although the watchful eyes and gossiping tongues were likely more benign in her case, she was no doubt talked about in her town

too. She was old and thought to be barren, but she was pregnant. The two women were bound by miracles. It made sense that Mary would rush to Elizabeth's side.

This joyous yet confusing time became even more joyous and confusing when the women met. Elizabeth felt her baby, who would grow up to be John the Baptist, jump in her womb at the sound of Mary's voice. But it was not the normal movements of an unborn child. Zechariah, John's father, had been told that John would be "filled with the Holy Spirit even before his birth" (Luke 1:15). When Elizabeth saw Mary, she realized that she was witness to the dawn of a new age. Affected by the Holy Spirit, she began to prophesize. Her response to the unborn Christ Child informs us as we also wait for Jesus. Elizabeth's four statements to Mary— recognition, declaration, joyous response, and faith—can guide us as we prepare ourselves for the birth of Jesus Christ.

Elizabeth's words recognized the incredible event that had happened to her relative. Mary was not married. For her, a pregnancy would be a sign of profound shame. But Elizabeth recognized holiness where it was least expected. Even though Mary was not visibly pregnant, Elizabeth immediately knew that Mary was carrying a blessed child. She saw a blessing when others would have seen tragedy. She recognized God's work where most would just see a troubled young girl.

As we prepare for the coming of Jesus, we must be able to recognize his work in the world today. The key is to be open to the presence of Jesus every moment in every day. If we only search for Jesus in the miraculous, we will miss seeing Jesus in the simple moments. Waiting for Jesus means that we are open to his arrival at any moment. If we are unable to recognize Jesus when he is present in our lives, we will be unable to welcome him and join in his work in the world.

Elizabeth then joyfully questioned why she would be so blessed by a visit from Mary. Notice Elizabeth's address for Mary in verse 43: "the mother of my Lord." Through Elizabeth's question, Luke offers the reader a central confession of Christian faith. Elizabeth names Jesus as her Lord even before his birth.

When you wait for a family member or friend at the airport, you see many other people arrive and be greeted by their loved ones. It is easy to recognize someone's father, mother, sibling, or spouse. But it is an entirely different feeling when your own loved one comes through the door. That person has a claim on your heart. To merely recognize Jesus is not enough. To be prepared for him means that you have declared Jesus as your own, and you have let him claim your heart.

Elizabeth declared Mary's unborn child as "my Lord." In doing so, she voiced a claim on her life. Because the child was her Lord, she was his willing servant. Naming Jesus as "my Lord" means entering into a covenant relationship, agreeing that God will be your God and you will be his follower. Advent means preparing yourself to welcome Jesus as your Lord and your Savior.

Next, Elizabeth explained the reason for John's jump of joy. John the Baptist was already fulfilling his calling as the one who would prepare the way for Jesus and announce him to the world. For Elizabeth and her own unborn child, the response to meeting Mary and her unborn child was absolute joy.

The Hebrew people had waited anxiously for centuries for the fulfillment of the promises for a Messiah and king. Under Roman rule, many believed that the Messiah would be a political ruler, freeing Israel from foreign dominance. But Jesus came for something even more profound. Jesus' kingdom promised peace and healing to broken hearts and souls and the freedom from the dominance of sin. Jesus' roles as both the shepherd king and sacrificial priest would be the dawning of an entirely new relationship with God, of a new covenant. When Jesus comes again, it will be for the final healing of the cosmos, and the establishment of the kingdom of God on earth. At that time, creation will finally be within the will of God, as it was created to be. It will be a time when humanity will reach its full potential, unencumbered by sin and evil. How could there be any other response to the coming of Jesus Christ other than a leap for joy?

Finally, Elizabeth blessed Mary for her faith. Mary heard and believed an amazing, impossible declaration from God—she was chosen to give birth to the Messiah. Not only that, Mary humbly and obediently accepted God's role for her, although it would turn her life upside down. Mary's trust and faith were a cause for celebration.

Following Jesus disrupts lives. Mary became pregnant before she was married. Fisherman left their nets by the shore. Beggars and blind men left their mats by the side of the road. Disciples stood with their mouths gaping at an empty tomb. The most certain things are no longer certain. Following Jesus takes boldness and courage. Faith means being willing to risk everything that the world offers and turn it over to God. Waiting for the return of Jesus Christ is not a passive activity. It is trusting that God will take and use our lives to his will and his honor and responding to his call with obedience for the kingdom of God.

Elizabeth's response to Mary and her unborn child, her Lord, demonstrated that she was prepared to meet the Messiah. As we prepare to meet Jesus Christ, may we also recognize his work in the world, confess his lordship in our lives, celebrate his gifts to us, and respond to him in obedience and faith. That is the work and the joy of the Advent season.

How does Elizabeth's recognition of Mary's unborn child inspire you to respond to Jesus as you prepare to celebrate his birth?

[1] From *http://www.warnersallman.com /collection/images/head-of-christ/*.
[2] From *An Introduction to The New Testament,* by Raymond E. Brown(Doubleday, 1997); page 684.
[3] Scripture quotations from THE MESSAGE. Copyright © by Eugene H. Peterson 1993, 1994, 1995, 1996, 2000, 2001, 2002. Used by permission of NavPress Publishing Group.
[4] From *The New Interpreter's Bible*, Vol. XII (Abingdon Press, 1998); page 11.

Welcome the Messiah

Scriptures for Christmas Eve:
Isaiah 9:2-7
Titus 2:11-14
Luke 2:1-20

The tree is up. The presents are wrapped. The house is decorated. But are you ready for Christmas?

Centuries ago, a poor young girl gave birth to the Messiah, and for those with eyes to see and ears to hear, the entire cosmos shifted. The barrier between heaven and earth was pushed open, and glimmers of the kingdom of God began to seep through. Those who noticed were invited to join in the light and were asked to focus and expand it with empowerment from above. We have a promise from God that this light will take over the entire world one day, and we will all be healed and made holy. The entire earth will be transformed.

On Christmas Eve, we celebrate the beginning of the end of the world as we know it. For Christians, the proper response to Christmas is to seek to transform into people of Christ's kingdom. Our celebration is not just for a baby who was born two thousand years ago; it is for the dawning of a new age in which we can join with God in confidence and joy and invest our lives in the kingdom of God. We celebrate that God has come to earth to live with us in our dirt and our pain to redeem us from our own mistakes and misdeeds. Our celebration is for the hope of today, which is our knowledge of Jesus Christ, the gift of the Holy Spirit, and the eventual healing of every pain, every wrong, every betrayal, and every sin forever.

To celebrate Christmas means to join in with joy. It means to count yourself as one of the people of the kingdom of God, ready and willing to spend your life serving God. It is a rededication to Christ's work and a renewal of hope for the future.

The world is yet to be redeemed, but Jesus Christ gave us a vision of how it will be. He healed the sick. He calmed the anxious. He fed the hungry. He tore down the barriers between God and human beings. He calls all people to be part of this vision of redemption.

HE WILL BE NAMED...
ISAIAH 9:2-7

Anyone who has heard the music of Handel's *Messiah* will recognize this Scripture. The words of joy and excitement about the birth of an amazing child reach through the ages to excite the hearts of Christians all over the world each Christmas. These words come to us from the prophet Isaiah.

The ministry and prophecy of Isaiah occurred about 700 years before Christ's birth. This passage was probably written soon after the Syro-Ephraimitic war (734 B.C.), a crisis that emerged for Judah because of the threat of an Assyrian advance. King Rezin of Damascus and King Pekah of Samaria formed a coalition and wanted King Ahaz of Judah to join them. When he refused, they moved against Judah, but they were unsuccessful in their efforts to dethrone Ahaz. Within a decade (722–721 B.C.), Assyria invaded the city of Samaria and resettled the people. The Northern Kingdom was destroyed. The Assyrian advance continued over the next few decades. Assyrians destroyed cities and towns in Judah and attacked Jerusalem in 701 B.C.; however, they withdrew without taking the city. This complex and terrifying history provides the background for Isaiah's prophecy.

Isaiah's views were rooted in the ancient belief that God had chosen David and his descendants to reign forever and to provide security for the people with a reign of justice and righteousness according to God's law (2 Samuel 7; Psalms 2; 89). When many kings failed to reign according to God's law, these ancient views came to be associated with an expectation for a Messiah, God's anointed ruler. Jerusalem was to be God's holy city that offered the promise of peace to all (Isaiah 2:1-4).

Isaiah 9:1-7 echoes the ancient vision of justice under a righteous king. Verses 6-7 celebrate the birth of a new crown prince, a descendant of David, who will reign "with justice and righteousness / now and forever." God delivers the people through this birth. While these words were intended for the people of Judah during the tumultuous events of the eighth century, Christians read these words and see God's justice and hope offered through Jesus Christ. The Gospel of Matthew refers to this Scripture at the beginning of Jesus' ministry when he made his home in Galilee. Matthew uses the same words to describe a spiritual awakening. In the same way, God's just and righteous king offered light during a time of darkness. Jesus' arrival is the dawn of a new age, bringing the light of God to all.

> the people who lived in the dark
>   have seen a great light,
>   and a light has come upon those
>   who lived in the region
>   and in shadow of death.

(Matthew 4:16)

It was custom in the ancient Near East for a newly crowned king to take on "throne names" that described characteristics of a perfect ruler. Such names praised the ruler's truth, wisdom, or valor. Verse 6 offers a litany of names that describe the attributes of God's just and righteous king, a king who is close to God and whose reign embraces and practices the nature of God. These names include Wonderful Counselor, Mighty God, Eternal Father, and Prince of Peace. The Hebrew word *ya'ats* is translated as "counselor" in verse 6, and it means to determine, advise, and guide. It is the description of a just and deliberate ruler. *Pele'*, which is translated as "wonderful," goes beyond a superlative to mean "miraculous." This king would be the wisest ruler the world has ever known.

Occasionally, rulers used "god" in their throne names to show that they were especially close to God. The people of Isaiah's time might have understood the name "Mighty God" to mean that God's power would be seen through this king. The throne name "Everlasting Father" carries a broad cluster of meanings. "Father" suggests one who creates, one who is the head of the household, and one who protects. The word "Everlasting" suggest one who is timeless. The name could also be translated as "Father of Perpetuity" or "Father of Eternity." This king will have a reign that will never end. Those of Isaiah's time might have under-

stood this to mean that the genealogical line of the king would continue forever, and his sons, grandsons, and great-grandsons would continue to be crowned. The last throne name is "Prince of Peace." For Isaiah's audience, who were fresh from the horrors of war, this title alone would be cause for celebration. "Peace" also suggests a well-being that includes completeness, soundness, and welfare. It describes the state of being that comes from a covenant relationship with God. We can always depend upon the one who creates, protects, and leads us forever.

As we wait for Jesus to come again, we may identify with the people of Judah and their ancestors. Our world is torn by war, hunger, and suffering. Illness, division, or financial stress may tear our families apart. Our hearts may be torn with resentment, shame, or fear. We prepare the way for God's anointed king by remembering Isaiah's words and reclaiming the hope they offer to us. Christians celebrate this hope in the birth of Jesus Christ. We can go to the Wonderful Counselor to heal the divisions in our lives. We can trust the power of the Mighty God. We can rest in the salvation of the Everlasting Father. The Prince of Peace can heal us. We can look forward in hope to the day when Jesus Christ will rule the world in justice and righteousness forever.

How do Isaiah's insights and visions of a just and righteous reign offer you hope for justice, righteousness, and peace in our world? How do you respond to the names listed in verse 6? How do they speak to you about God's presence in your daily life?

LIVING IN CHRIST TODAY
TITUS 2:11-14

The Scriptures of Jesus' birth and second coming are exciting and inspiring. What does all this mean to us right now, today? How does God want us to respond?

This lectionary passage in Titus is found after one of the four passages in the New Testament known as *Haustafel,* or household codes (Ephesians 5:21–6:9; Colossians 3:18–4:1; Titus 2:1-10; 1 Peter 2:18–3:7). They are some of the most controversial Scriptures in the New Testament because they outline proper behavior between husbands and wives, children and their parents, and slaves and their masters. Obviously, there are vast differences in culture and attitudes between the ancient Near East and the United States today, and the specific instructions in the household codes are not all relevant for life in the 21st century. But all examples of *Haustafel* have a common theme—treating one another with love and respect. Titus 2:11-14 explains why people should live by the household codes and offers theological reasoning behind instructions for Christian living.

And how are Christians to live now? We are in the tension be-tween the work that Jesus began on earth and the promised fulfill-ment in the future. The Messiah has come, but we are still waiting for him. The Kingdom has dawned, but it is not here. Our lives have been changed, but we are still the same. Our hearts have been trans-formed, but we still sin.

Titus 2:11-12 sets the stage: "The grace of God has appeared, bring-ing salvation to all people. It edu-cates us so that we can live sensible, ethical, and godly lives right now." It is because we live in the time between Jesus' life on earth and his second coming that we need to examine and adjust our behaviors. Through God's grace in Christ, we have been given salvation. God's grace guides and educates us in right behavior. We have the power of Christ, the guidance of the Holy Spirit, and the knowledge of our own redemption, which teaches us how to behave toward others if we listen. Through Christ, we have been given a vision of righteous-ness, which is the kingdom of God. Because Christ has conquered sin and death, Christ's people have the hope and power to live as reflections of Christ in the world.

Titus 2:13 is a significant verse because it leaves no doubt about the identity of the redeemer. Jesus is referred to as "our great God and savior." Jesus is the Messiah, God incarnate. He is no less than the almighty God who gave him-self to liberate us from our sins. But liberation from sin does not mean liberation from human nature. Even the most devout Christians still find themselves behaving badly at times. Although we have the gift of God's grace and Christ's salvation, the world has not been healed. We are still waiting for Christ's reign on earth, and living in the meantime is not always easy. But as Christ's followers, our actions are to be the glimmers of the Kingdom that others can see. We are to reflect the hope of Jesus Christ that will one day renew and reconcile the world.

Conversion and salvation are not things that happen only within a person's soul. Spiritual studies and the resulting deep theological insights are valuable but not the only mark of a Christian. Even the most profound theology is flawed if it does not translate into a guide for life. Faith becomes suspect if a person is thoughtless and irritable towards family, friends, and acquaintances. Looking inward can sometimes blind someone from looking outward.

One of the common criticisms of Christians is that they do not behave differently than anyone else. Christians can be just as thoughtless, cruel, and mean as other people. These may be the same people who go to church every week, study their Bibles daily, and profess a strong faith. They—and we—may believe that we are living lives of love. Those familiar with us (friends, family, and neighbors) deal with our irritation and bad moods. Thus, living in Christian love is pushed further away

from our daily lives to the periphery where it becomes a special event rather than a habit. Those who live and work with us may see little evidence of our faith.

This is why the household codes are still relevant. Even though we would not follow the specific directions of behavior—for example, we now realize that slavery is abhorrent—the codes remind us that Christian living is a daily exercise in Christ-like love towards all people, all the time. Jesus does not love us because we are inherently lovable. When he came to earth, he was reviled, betrayed, and put to death, but he still continues to reach out in love. Jesus commands us in John 15:12 to "love each other just as I have loved you." The way Jesus acts toward us is our guide for how we should act toward others. This is not a patronizing, teeth-gritting kind of love, but a love that flows from the grace and power of Jesus Christ. It is through his grace and power that we can have this kind of love toward others. This is what Jesus came to teach us. Titus 2:14 tells us that Christ came to earth to cleanse us and to excite us to do good in the world.

Every year, there are countless magazine and web articles about how to survive family gatherings during the holidays. Tips include taking breaks from the crowd, putting some subjects off limits for discussion, and silently repeating the phrase, "This only happens once a year." But these gatherings are opportunities to show what it means to be a Christian. Christ came to redeem us so that we would actually be eager to be the peacemakers and the healers. The grace of God is here to train us to be "sensible, ethical and godly" right now while we wait for completeness in Christ (verse 12).

In what concrete ways can you demonstrate your faith and Christian love to your family and friends this Christmas? to others in your life?

GOD WITH US
LUKE 2:1-20

I have had the good fortune to travel around the world, and I have seen many glorious cathedrals. The spires are breathtaking, and the spaces inside are reverent and awe-inspiring, often encrusted with gold and silver. These are the places that human beings have created to commune with God.

But when God entered the world as a human being, he was not in a holy and reverent place, but probably in a noisy, crowded peasant home surrounded by animals. Traditionally, the translation of Luke 2:7 states that there was no room for Mary and Joseph in the inn, and people have assumed that Jesus was born in a stable because of the reference to a manger. However, careful examination of the Greek words coupled with archeological evidence of peasant homes of the era lead to a different con-

clusion. Luke 2:7 uses the word *katalyma,* which can mean "guest chamber," "dining room," or "eating room." In contrast, the word *pandocheion,* which refers to a commercial inn, is the word used in the story of the good Samaritan (Luke 10:25-37). Very few people of that era had separate housing for animals and instead brought them into an area of the home that was dug lower than the family living quarters every evening for safekeeping. Therefore, Jesus was most likely born in a busy, crowded peasant home in which his parents were not even the most important guests. The only safe place for the newborn infant was in the feeding trough of the animals, which was usually a depression dug into the raised part of the floor.

This was not a beautiful, outwardly holy place but a spot in the very midst of humanity. Crèches from the Catalonian region of Spain often include a small figure called a *caganer* in the background, relieving himself.[1] While it is crude, it illustrates an important point. The Messiah and Savior of the world did not enter the world as a king in material glory and honor but in the messy, crude, and human circumstances of the world. Jesus did not live above even the most basic dirt of the earth. The Son of God came as a poor Jewish child squeezed into a peasant home as an unimportant guest. In contrast to the breathtaking cathedrals built in his honor, Jesus chose to meet humanity in a manger, surrounded by the nitty-gritty elements of the world.

God chose to have a birth announcement. Kings would send poets and orators out into the villages to announce the birth of a new prince. This time, the poets came from heaven. God sent a choir of angels to announce the birth of Jesus, but they were not sent to priests or government officials. They were sent to menial workers, shepherds, who were alone in the fields with their sheep. Shepherds connected the newborn to David, the shepherd king.

The birth narrative in Luke is so familiar to us that it can be difficult to hear it in a fresh, new way. However, just try to imagine those shepherds in the night. They were probably sitting down together in the dark, maybe dozing a little, chatting quietly as they watched the sheep. Then came a blinding light, and within it, an angel. The sheep must have scattered, but the shepherds were transfixed, trembling. Angels in the Bible are not the chubby little cherubs we often see in paintings. In Scripture, people are often terrified at the sight of them. However, the angel who spoke to the shepherds calmed them. The angel came to deliver good news of great joy. Great joy would replace great fear. This message was for the entire world. From the very beginning, Jesus was not just a Messiah for the Jews, but for every person on the planet.

The angel's message is a study in Luke's Christology. Bethlehem was identified as the city of David, which linked Jesus to the Davidic covenant, God's promise that a descendent of David would be on Israel's throne forever. The angel also named Jesus as a savior, or deliverer. To the tired ears of oppressed people, it might have sounded as though Jesus would be a political hero, but we know that the angel was referring to Jesus' death and resurrection. He would be savior of the souls of the world. The angel then announced Jesus as "Christ the Lord," a name for Jesus that is not anywhere else in the New Testament. *Christ* is the Greek word for "Messiah," but like Elizabeth's declaration, the angel calls the infant "the Lord." This tiny baby, lying in a feeding trough in a non-descript village, is the Lord God.

The way to identify the correct baby must have been a shock because it was so common. Babies were traditionally swaddled at birth and nearly every peasant home had a manger. Just as the shepherds puzzled about the unexceptional sign, an angel chorus appeared, singing praises and glory to God in heaven. When God is glorified, the earth is blessed with peace. This moment was the beginning of the eschatological promise of the healing of the world. Christ's presence on the planet would usher in God's will on earth as it is in heaven. With this miraculous birth, the world could finally see glimmers of the kingdom of God.

The shepherds decided to enter the village and find the infant. Although the sign from the angel was not specific, Bethlehem was small enough that even a normal birth was probably news. Until the shepherds arrived, Mary and Joseph were completely unaware that the heavens were rejoicing at Jesus' birth. For others in the town, perhaps the shepherds' witness could have been dismissed since they were not influential in the community. But Mary understood. She grasped the implications not only for her life but also for the entire world. This child was indeed the Messiah. Christ the Savior was born.

Few of us have homes fit for a king. It doesn't matter. The King of the world came to the home of a common peasant. Few of us have the means to welcome God with the splendor he deserves. It doesn't matter. The infant Jesus was wrapped in bands of cloth like any other newborn and laid to sleep in a feeding trough. Few of us have the credentials or credibility to announce a new world order. It doesn't matter. God first gave that task to the outcasts, shepherds. What does matter is that we recognize what this child means and understand the profound difference that his life had—and will have—on us. It matters that we accept the salvation that he was born to bring. It matters that we name him as our Lord. It matters that we spend our lives listening to him and obeying him so that glimmers of his kingdom will be on earth as it is in heaven. And it matters that we eagerly anticipate his second coming when the cosmos will be transformed, bringing every heart and mind within the peace and glory of our Lord and Savior.

How do you respond to the humble circumstances of Jesus' birth? What does the narrative say to you about God's willingness to be born in the realities of our everyday lives?

---

[1] From *http://www.chicagotribune.com/features/ct-caganer-pg,0,3838936.photogallery.*

$\mathscr{L}$EADER GUIDE

HOW TO LEAD THIS STUDY

Preparing the Way invites adults to explore and reflect upon the Revised Common Lectionary Bible readings for the season of Advent. This Advent study is rooted in the texts for Year C of the three-year lectionary cycle of readings. Each week you will find readings from the Old Testament, the Epistles, and a Gospel. "How to Lead This Study" guides you in setting up and leading the study. You'll discover tips for preparing for each week's session, as well as ideas about how to successfully lead a Bible study, even if you have never led one before. Although the Revised Common Lectionary designates a psalm or words of praise for each week, they are generally not discussed in the main content. These additional Scriptures are, however, listed here along with ideas for incorporating them into the session. "How to Lead This Study" offers some historical and theological information about the season of Advent and suggests ways that people now and in different times and places have observed this sacred time. In addition, you will find prayers and a selection of hymns appropriate for each week's session.

About Advent

Advent is the first season in the twelve-month cycle of seasons in the church known as the liturgical year. *Advent* is from a Latin word that means "coming." This definition is fitting, for during the season of Advent we await the coming of Christ. We look in two directions for this coming: backward in time to recall the birth of Jesus Christ in Bethlehem and forward as we anticipate his return of the King of kings and Lord of lords. In Western churches, the season begins four weeks prior to Christmas on the Sunday closest to November 30th and ends on Christmas Eve. Altars have traditionally been adorned in purple, the color of royalty that reminds us of Christ's sovereignty. Purple is also associated with penitence, which is appropriate for this season because historically Advent, like Lent, has been a time to reflect and repent. More recently, blue has been favored in many churches because of its association with Mary, who artists often depict wearing blue. Just as Mary waited for the birth of her holy Child, so the church eagerly awaits his coming.

Advent is a time of preparation. However, some churches rush headlong into Christmas, skipping over this important time to get ready. Even on the first week of Advent, Christmas carols ring out. Nativity scenes feature the Magi, whose arrival is celebrated on January 6th, which is Epiphany. Actually, Christmas is a separate season of twelve days. Although the secular world may push us toward Christmas, in the church we take the time to prepare ourselves for Christ's coming and coming again.

Advent has the potential to form and transform us if we allow that to happen. As we wait expectantly for the One God called Son, we bump up against the realities of the world with all its suffering, injustice, and hostility. Yet if we consider the scriptural promises of this season, we know that God is at work among us and within us to change not only ourselves but also the world. We live in the space between the first and second coming of Christ. God's realm has broken in upon us with Jesus' birth; it will appear in its fullness when he returns. In the interim, we live as Advent people who keep alert and constantly prepare for his coming.

Ways to Celebrate Advent

The season of Advent provides time for us to get ready for the coming—and coming again—of our Lord Jesus Christ. During this season of preparation, many people attend special study groups, just as you are doing, to discover what the Savior's coming is all about and what he means in their lives. People use Advent wreaths and Advent calendars as two means of personal spiritual growth. Another way to celebrate the season, setting up an angel tree, involves sharing resources with those in need.

ADVENT WREATHS: Many sanctuaries, Sunday school rooms, and homes are adorned with Advent wreaths. Thought to have first been used in northern Europe, wreath traditions have varied, but by the 16th century, the wreath had taken on the form that we recognize today. The roundness of the wreath and the evergreens used to create it symbolize life. Traditionally, three purple candles are lit on the first, second, and fourth Sundays. A rose-colored candle, symbolizing joy, is lit on the third Sunday. More recently, blue candles are used for all four weeks. Some wreaths include a center white candle, which is lit late on Christmas Eve to symbolize Christ.

ADVENT CALENDARS: Originating in Germany in the late 1800's, Advent calendars provide a way to count down the days until Christmas, beginning on December 1. The calendar includes twenty-four small windows that each hide a picture. Although early calendars used images from the Old Testament, contemporary ones frequently display items that appeal to children, such as teddy bears or candy.

ANGEL TREES: Some churches and other organizations decorate trees using angels, which are often made of construction paper. Listed on the angels are items that an individual or family in need would like to have for Christmas. Generally these lists include food, clothing (with sizes and colors indicated), and toys. Social-services agencies or schools usually provide lists. Those who choose to participate select an angel, purchase the requested items, and return them by the date specified on the angel. Some organizations ask that the gifts be wrapped; others prefer to wrap all gifts in a central location. Either way, gifts need to be marked using the number or code shown on the angel. A group of helpers delivers the gifts, usually on December 23rd or 24th.

Organize an Advent Study Group

Advent is an especially busy time of year for most people. Yet, it is also a time when Christians yearn to deepen their relationship with Christ. Study groups are an excellent way to enable people to delve deeper into the Bible and to reach out in friendship to others. Established groups—Sunday school classes, current Bible study groups, men's or women's groups—may choose to focus on Advent. Also consider forming a new group for this five-week Advent study. By advertising the study in local media, you can open wide the doors of the church to include those who may not currently attend your congregation.

When you, in conjunction with the pastor and church education team, have determined the shape of the group, decide when and where they can meet. An established group would most likely continue to meet in its regular space and time. A new group will have to be scheduled so as not to conflict with other activities that potential participants would likely attend, such as choir rehearsal. Evening meetings are more likely to pull in individuals who are still working, whereas daytime meetings may be more attractive to older adults who choose not to be out after dark, full-time moms, and college students. The time of the meeting will suggest whether refreshments are needed. A Saturday morning is a good time to offer a continental breakfast. A noon meeting could include the invitation to bring a bag lunch. An evening meeting might include some light snacks and beverages.

The learning space should be large enough for the group you anticipate. A Sunday school room with tables would be ideal. Since many churches conserve energy by regulating individual room temperatures, request that the room be properly heated by the time the participants arrive and remain so during the meeting time. Make sure that a small worship table and large writing surface, such as an easel with large sheets of paper and markers, a markerboard with markers, or a blackboard with chalk will be on hand. Have a separate space available and a designated worker to provide childcare.

Decide whether you want to hold a preregistration. Whether you do or not, be sure to order enough copies of *Preparing the Way* so that each participant has the study book. The church will need to determine how much to charge participants or whether to underwrite the cost and announce that the study is free.

Prepare for the Sessions

Leading a Bible study is a sacred privilege. Before you begin the "nuts-and-bolts" work, pray for the Holy Spirit to guide you and the participants as you encounter each week's Bible passages. Try reading each Scripture devotionally by asking God to speak to your heart through a word or phrase that grabs your attention. Meditate on whatever you are shown and allow this idea to shape your own spiritual growth.

Read the Scriptures and Bible Background for each week's lesson to understand the context of the Scriptures and their meaning. If time permits, consult other commentaries to expand your knowledge. Once you feel comfortable with the Scriptures, begin to plan the session by following these steps:

1. Read the session plan from *Preparing the Way*.
2. Refer to the Session Plan where you will find suggested activities for opening the session, for each of the Scriptures, and for closing the session. Decide which of these activities will work best with your group. Choose one activity from each of the five sections. Be aware that the activities generally include discussion, but some include art, music, movement, or other means of learning in addition to discussion.
3. If you choose activities that refer directly to *Preparing the Way*, mark the places in your book for easy reference during the session.
4. Gather supplies for the selected activities. You will find the supplies listed at the beginning of each activity.
5. Select the hymn(s) you wish to use. If you will sing the hymn(s), notify your accompanist.
6. Determine how you will use the lectionary psalm or other additional reading.
7. Contact any guest speakers or assistants early in the week if you will use their services.

Helpful Ideas for Leading a Group

Bible studies come in many shapes, sizes, and formats. Some begin with a theme and find biblical support for it. Others begin with the Bible itself and unpack the Scriptures, whether from one book or several. Our study begins with the Bible, specifically the texts of the Revised Common Lectionary. Those Scriptures will deeply inform our study. However, *Preparing the Way* is not a "verse by verse" study of the readings. Instead, we are studying the texts as a kind of roadmap to guide us in our spiritual journey through the Advent season. Consequently, some of the suggested activities call participants to struggle with questions of faith in their own lives. Our focus is primarily on transformation so that participants may grow in their relationship with Jesus Christ and become more closely conformed to his image. That's a tall order for a five-week course! And it may be somewhat challenging for the participants, since it may be far easier to discuss historical information about the Bible and consider various interpretations of a passage than it is to wrestle with what the passage says to me—personally and as a member of the body of Christ—in contemporary life.

Your role as the leader of this group is to create an environment in which participants will feel safe raising their questions and expressing their doubts. You can also help the class feel comfortable by making clear that you rely solely on volunteers to answer questions and to read aloud. If adults feel pressed to respond or read, they may be embarrassed and may not return to the group. If questions arise that you can definitely answer, do so. If you do not know the answer but suspect that an answer is available, say you do not know and offer to look it up and report back at the next session. Or suggest a type of resource that will likely include the answer and challenge the questioner and others to do some research and report back. Some questions cannot be fully answered—at least not in this life. Do not be afraid to point out that people through the ages have wrestled with some questions, yet they remain mysteries. If you can truly say so, respond that you have wrestled with that same question and have found an answer that works for you or that you are still searching. When you show yourself to be a co-learner, the participants will feel more comfortable than if you act as the all-knowing expert. You will feel more at ease about leading the group as well.

Additional Scriptures for Advent

The additional Scriptures for this season come from the Psalms, Luke, and Isaiah. Suggestions are given in each session for using these Scriptures, but you may want to try other options. For example, consider reading each psalm responsively, possibly adding the sung response if you are using the Psalter in your hymnal. Notice that two of the additional Scriptures come from Luke. Some hymnals, such as *The United Methodist Hymnal,* include responsive readings with sung responses for Mary's "Magnificat" (*UMH,* 199) and Zechariah's benediction (*UMH,* 208). For the reading from Isaiah 12 on the Third Sunday of Advent, you may want to select a volunteer to read the passage from his or her Bible.

First Sunday of Advent: Psalm 25:1-10
Second Sunday of Advent: Luke 1:68-79
Third Sunday of Advent: Isaiah 12:2-6
Fourth Sunday of Advent: Luke 1:46b-55
Christmas Eve: Psalm 96

Prayers for Advent

Suggestions for using these weekly prayers are found in their respective sessions.

First Sunday of Advent: God of the Ages, as we look back to celebrate your coming in the flesh, we also look ahead to the day when your kingdom will come in all its fullness as Christ returns. Help us to keep alert for the signs of his coming. Empower us to live each day so we may stand with upraised heads when he appears on that great and terrifying day. We pray through our Lord Jesus Christ, who with you and the Holy Spirit lives and reigns forever. Amen.[1]

Second Sunday of Advent: Holy One of Israel, just as the refiner can see his reflection in purified silver, may others be able to see the Messiah in us.

Let us closely follow the example of Christ, who humbled himself to do your will, no matter what the cost. Empower us to announce his coming so that others may seek your salvation. We pray through our Lord Jesus Christ, who with you and the Holy Spirit lives and reigns forever. Amen.

Third Sunday of Advent: Precious Lord, we lift our prayers of praise and thanksgiving, knowing that you are near to us. Empower us to live as your children, caring for those in need and seeking the common good for all. Grant us your peace, which far exceeds our understanding, so that our hearts and minds will rest safely in your beloved Son. We pray through our Lord Jesus Christ, who with you and the Holy Spirit lives and reigns forever. Amen.

Fourth Sunday of Advent: Loving Father, whose Son is the exact imprint of your own being, we give thanks for the many ways we can envision the Beloved One. We are blessed to know him as the tender shepherd, the high priest who sacrificed himself for our sake and continually makes intercession on our behalf, and the vulnerable baby who was formed in Mary's womb to live among us. We pray through our Lord Jesus Christ, who with you and the Holy Spirit lives and reigns forever. Amen.

Christmas Eve: Great God our Savior, we worship and adore you as we again celebrate your arrival this Christmas Eve. Like the shepherds who heard the angels sing, may we drop everything and hurry to welcome you. Let us follow their example in telling others the good news of the birth of the Messiah. We pray through our Lord Jesus Christ, who with you and the Holy Spirit lives and reigns forever. Amen.

Hymns for Advent

Each week you have a choice of three hymns appropriate for the season of Advent—one related to the Old Testament lesson, one to the Epistle, and one to the Gospel. Select hymns based on the Scripture you want to highlight or the familiarity of the hymn to the group. You may wish to sing an entire hymn or only selected verses. If you choose to use music in more than one activity, sing the hymn in one activity and read a different hymn in unison or responsively for another activity. You may also choose to use the lyrics of the hymns as the basis for a discussion about a particular Advent theme.

First Sunday of Advent
Old Testament: "Blessed Be the God of Israel"
Epistle: "Where Charity and Love Prevail"
Gospel: "Come, Thou Long-Expected Jesus"

Second Sunday of Advent
Old Testament: "Toda la Tierra" ("All Earth Is Waiting")
Epistle: "More Love to Thee, O Christ"
Gospel: "O Come, O Come, Emmanuel"

Third Sunday of Advent
Old Testament: "Send Your Word"
Epistle: "Rejoice, the Lord Is King"
Gospel: "In the Bleak Midwinter"

Fourth Sunday of Advent
Old Testament: "Once in Royal David's City"
Epistle: "What Does the Lord Require"
Gospel: "Lo, How a Rose E'er Blooming"

Christmas Eve
Old Testament: "Arise, Shine Out, Your Light Has Come"
Epistle: "Joy to the World"
Gospel: "Angels We Have Heard on High"

1. Thy Kingdom Come

BIBLE BACKGROUND

Jeremiah 33:14-16

The Book of Jeremiah reflects a period of political, social, and economic upheaval in Judah, also known as the Southern Kingdom. In 597 B.C., Judah revolted against the dominant power of the day, Babylon. In response, Babylon invaded Judah in 597 B.C. and again in 587 B.C., this time not only carting off the inhabitants, but also destroying the city and Temple. Those who were deported remained in exile in Babylon until 539 B.C. when the Persian king Cyrus, who had defeated the Babylonians, decreed that the Israelites could return home and rebuild the Temple (Ezra 1:1-4). During this period of captivity, the question of Israel's relationship with God loomed over these captives who had no hope.

Although much of the material found in Jeremiah sounds a tone of doom and despair, today's passage is taken from the small collection of poetry and prose found in Jeremiah 30:1–33:26, known as "the little book of consolation." In the midst of life-altering turmoil, God commanded Jeremiah to write words of hope to the people. The immediate future would not change, but "the time is coming" (33:14) when God would fulfill promises by restoring the Davidic monarchy. The "righteous branch" (verse 15), to be known as "The LORD Is Our Righteousness" (verse 16), will be a ruler whose reign is marked by actions that are "just and right" (verse 15).

God's promise, though unfulfilled at the time of Jeremiah's writing, was meant to console the people. Their future would be very different from the one they were experiencing in Babylon. While that may have seemed difficult to fathom, if they could recall the many situations in which God provided for them in the past, they could imagine a new and different future. Unlike their current situation under an oppressive ruler, the people would enjoy life under one who ruled with justice and righteousness. But they would have to wait for that One to come. As Christians, we believe that One is Jesus, whose coming and coming again we also await during Advent.*

1 Thessalonians 3:9-13

During his second missionary journey, Paul and his companion Silas visited Thessalonica (Acts 17:1-9). For "three Sabbaths" (verse 2), they preached in a synagogue. Jews, devout Gentiles, and some prominent women chose to join Paul and Silas. Displeased with Paul's message, some among the Jews enlisted the help of "thugs" (verse 5) to create an uproar. They made a politically explosive claim that the two missionaries had preached that someone other than Caesar—Jesus—was king (verse 7).

After leaving Thessalonica, Paul sent Timothy to encourage this church. He also wrote a letter to the believers in about A.D. 50. Most scholars consider 1 Thessalonians to be the oldest portion of the New Testament. Although Timothy's report about this congregation was generally glowing, there was apparently something lacking in their faith (1 Thessalonians 3:10). Paul prayed fervently that he would be able to return and help this congregation, who he addressed as family, to complete their faith.

In the benediction of verses 11-13, Paul asked that God increase the love among the members so that they would be well prepared for the (second) coming of Christ. Paul longed for them to be "blameless in holiness" (verse 13) when Christ returned. The apostle himself modeled this kind of love when he bid their love to enrich one another "in the same way as we also love you" (verse 12).

Paul's words were directed to a congregation who wondered about the return of Christ—and what would happen to those who died before that event. We too live in the time between Christ's first and second coming. As such, Paul's words are equally appropriate and useful for us. We must continue to live in the tension created by the "already" and "not yet." To do that, we, like the Thessalonians, must live reflecting God's love even as we look ahead to an unknown time when Christ will return to reign as King of kings and Lord of lords.*

Luke 21:25-36

Just before the plot to kill Jesus crystalized in Luke 22, Jesus talked in Chapter 21 about persecution and the destruction of the Temple in Jerusalem. Cataclysmic events will occur not only on earth but also in all creation. Foreboding signs in the heavens, on the seas, and among the nations will herald the return of Christ. His coming will create fear, but his followers will "stand up straight . . . because [their] redemption is near" (verse 28).

Jesus wanted his followers to be prepared for these events and so he told a parable about a fig tree. The leaves of the tree are signs of summer, just as surely as the cosmic signs Jesus referred to are signs of his return. Luke 21:32 is problematic, for it seems to say that those who hear Jesus speaking will be alive when the end comes. Yet the meaning is ambiguous, perhaps referring to the "generation" alive when the signs first appear. However this verse is interpreted, Jesus assured us that his words "will certainly not pass away" (verse 33).

As was true in our readings from Jeremiah and 1 Thessalonians, here again there is a period of waiting for promises to be fulfilled. In Acts 1:9-11, two heavenly messengers told the witnesses to Jesus' ascension that he would return "in the same way that you saw him go into heaven" (verse 11). Jesus made clear in Luke 21:34-36 that this in-between time was not to be frittered away or lived carelessly. Instead, his people are to live in the expectation of his return. Believers are called to beware, to "stay alert at all times" (verse 36). To keep alert, Christ's followers are to pray for strength during this time of unprecedented turmoil. They are to be ready and faithful at all times, for the timing of these events is unknown even to Jesus himself, according to Mark 13:32. In contrast to those who are prepared, those who are not ready will be "dulled by drinking parties, drunkenness, and the anxieties of day-to-day life" (Luke 21:34). The way we conduct ourselves day by day, moment by moment, has far-reaching consequences.

LEARNING MENU

To begin the Advent journey.

Introduce participants to each other and to the study

Supplies: Preparing the Way, nametags, markers

Welcome each participant and distribute *Preparing the Way*. Invite participants to make a nametag and introduce themselves to those who they do not know. If there are newcomers to an established group, be certain that everyone is introduced and welcomed.

Turn to the two sections in "How to Lead This Study" titled "About Advent" and "Ways to Celebrate Advent." Read or retell these sections. End by encouraging participants to talk about other ways they celebrate Advent. Some of these ways may reflect cultural or ethnic traditions, whereas others may be customs that a particular family observes during Advent.

Ask a volunteer to read "Introduction" in *Preparing the Way*. Conclude by encouraging participants to talk about strategies they use to promote spiritual growth as they wait for the coming of Christ during Advent. Point out that attending this Bible study is one very helpful strategy.

To recognize that "The LORD Is Our Righteousness"
(Jeremiah 33:14-16).

A   Analyze the story

Supplies: Bibles, Preparing the Way, large sheet of paper, marker

Read or retell the Bible Background for Jeremiah. Ask a volunteer to read Jeremiah 33:14-16 as the other participants follow along in their Bibles. Discuss these questions, either with all the participants or in smaller teams if the total group is large. If you plan to form discussion teams, write the following questions on a large sheet of paper prior to the session: What events led up to the Israelites' current situation in Babylon? Had you been one of the exiles, what questions would you have had about God? Before hearing Jeremiah's words in Chapter 33, what would have been your expectation of the future? How might your expectations have changed after hearing Jeremiah? What meaning does this passage have for you as a 21st century Christian as you await the coming and coming again of Jesus Christ?

B   Explore God's promise as an antidote to human despair

Supplies: Bibles, Preparing the Way

Help the participants to imagine the situation of the exiles in Babylon by retelling information from the Bible Background for Jeremiah and the section titled "The LORD Is Our Righteousness." Invite the participants to comment on how they might have felt had they been among the exiles.

Enlist a volunteer to read Jeremiah 33:14-16. Encourage the participants to comment on how these words might have changed their attitudes, though not the reality of their situation, had they been in Babylon.

Choose someone to read the paragraph from *Preparing the Way* that begins "Hope in God is never cruel or false." Point out that people who are in despair need to be able to find hope. Ask: What are some reasons that people today may feel hopeless? How might Jeremiah's words bring hope to the hopeless today? In what ways do you think God's promise of a righteous ruler can bring hope to our lives?

C Create roleplays

Supplies: Bibles, Preparing the Way

Set the stage by inviting a volunteer to read three paragraphs from *Preparing the Way,* beginning with "The city of Jerusalem was shattered" and ending with "the highest hill of Jerusalem." Mention that the apparent breaking of long-standing covenantal promises caused the people to doubt their relationship with God and God's future for them.

Choose someone to read Jeremiah 33:14-16. Notice that "the time is coming" (verse 14) when God will raise up a "righteous branch" (verse 15) from the line of David, but there is a period of waiting that will precede the fulfillment of that promise—and the length of that period is unknown.

Form several groups to roleplay a discussion among the exiles as they consider what Jeremiah's prophecy means to them. Suggest that they try to imagine what it will be like to await the fulfillment of God's promised ruler from David's line. Allow each group time to present their roleplay to the entire group.

To see glimmers of God's kingdom
(1 Thessalonians 3:9-13).

A Learn about the church in Thessalonica

Supplies: Bibles, Preparing the Way, map

Select a volunteer to read 1 Thessalonians 3:9-13. Locate Thessalonica on a map. Relate Paul's experiences in Thessalonica by reading the Bible Background for this Scripture.

Form several small teams and assign each team two or three paragraphs from information in *Preparing the Way* for "Glimmers of the Kingdom." Each team is to read its assignment and be ready to report one or two key ideas. Call everyone together and hear their brief reports.

Discuss these questions: The members of the Thessalonian church were on the margins of their society because of their relationship with Christ. What glimmers of hope might Paul's proclamation and prayer have offered to them? Based on this short passage, how would you describe Paul's relationship with this church? What similarities can you discern between the church in Thessalonica and the exiles in Babylon? What similarities can you discern between the church in Thessalonica and members of Christian churches around the world today? What glimmers of hope can you see as you await the coming and coming again of God's kingdom as it appears to us in Christ?

B   Reflect on a complete faith

Supplies: Bibles, large sheet of paper, marker

Enlist a volunteer to read 1 Thessalonians 3:9-13. Tell participants that Timothy gives a glowing report about this congregation that Paul founded—except for the fact that their faith is not yet complete. Yet, he does not give specific examples as to why someone's faith would be incomplete, or how he defines completeness. He does indicate, however, that this faith is holy and that the one who exhibits such faith is "blameless" (verse 13), loving, and, therefore, well prepared for the coming again of Christ.

Brainstorm answers to the following question, listing ideas on a large sheet of paper: What actions or attitudes suggest a mature, complete faith in God? Provide a few moments for participants to reflect on this list, making a mental note of those characteristics that they feel they possess and those that they would like to develop. Encourage each person to pray silently that they as individuals and your church as a body will have such a complete faith. Conclude by reading Paul's benediction from verses 11-13 as a heartfelt prayer for the entire congregation.

C   Express God's love to others

Supplies: Bibles, slips of paper, pencils, basket (or other small container)

Select a volunteer to read 1 Thessalonians 3:9-13. Ask: What effect do you think has this congregation's love for Paul and their love for one another had on both Paul and the congregation?

Distribute a slip of paper and a pencil to each person. Invite each person to complete this sentence on the paper: I experience God's love for me when other members of the congregation _____. Pass around a basket or other small container. Prompt participants to drop their signed papers into the container and then return it to you. Encourage participants to listen for ways that they might show God's love to those in this group. Read the sentences aloud. Finish by challenging each person to take at least one caring action for someone else during this Advent season.

To realize the importance of being alert and prepared for Christ's coming (Luke 21:25-36).

A Explore Jesus' teaching on his coming again

Supplies: Bibles, Preparing the Way

Choose three volunteers, one to read Luke 21:25-28, a second for verses 29-33, and a third for verses 34-36. Invite participants to scan the section titled "Be Alert and Prepared" in *Preparing the Way*. Discuss these questions: What do we mean by the word *apocalypse*? What do other Gospel writers have to say about an apocalypse? (If time permits, ask several participants to read aloud the accounts noted in Matthew and Mark.) What do other prophecies mentioned in this section add to the idea of apocalypse? What does Jesus call his followers to do during the time that we await these events? What difference might the news of an apocalypse make in relation to our expectations for the future? What difference might this news make as to how the church lives today in the world?

B Draw a meaningful image

Supplies: Bibles, Preparing the Way, unlined paper, pencils

Invite participants to close their eyes and envision the images as you read Luke 21:25-36. Distribute paper and pencils and encourage them to draw one or two images that stood out for them. Make clear that artistic ability is unimportant. What we are looking for is an image that made an impression.

Encourage participants to scan the section titled "Be Alert and Prepared" in *Preparing the Way* to find information pertaining to the images they selected. Suggest that participants work with a partner or in small teams to show and talk about the images they chose. Have them discuss the following questions: Why did the image(s) capture your attention? What thoughts or feelings did it evoke? What does this image reveal about the end time? How might the remembrance of this image help you to better prepare for Christ's coming?

C Create an Advent poster

Supplies: Bibles, art supplies for a poster (such as posterboard or construction paper, markers, scissors, glue, glitter)

Read Luke 21:25-36 as dramatically as possible. Point out that Jesus called his followers to "stay alert at all times" (verse 36). Although neither we nor he (see Mark 13:32) know when he will come again, Jesus taught us that signs can help us to be aware of the time. Specifically, he referred to the sprouting of the leaves of a fig tree.

Set out art supplies. Depending upon the size of the group, individuals may each want to make a poster or several participants may choose to work together. Suggest that they use a tree as their symbol for this poster. Also suggest that they write words from Luke 21 or Matthew 13 to help those who see the posters better understand this Advent message of being alert to the signs of Christ's coming.

Display these posters in areas of the church where people of all ages are likely to see them. Several participants may remain after the session to take these posters to various locations in the building.

To go forth on the Advent journey.

Worship Together

Supplies: paper, pencil, hymnals or Bibles

Thank everyone for their participation. Suggest that they read Chapter 2 in *Preparing the Way* prior to the next session.

Read Psalm 25:1-10 responsively from a hymnal with a Psalter. Consider using a sung response for Advent if your hymnal includes one. If your hymnal does not include a Psalter, invite one person to read verses 1-5 from the Bible and a second person to read verses 6-10.

Invite participants to pair off with someone who is not a family member or close friend. These two people are to act as prayer partners for one another during the course of this Advent study. Distribute paper and pencils so that each pair may swap contact information and discern the best time and way to get in touch with one another. Provide time for the partners to get to know each other and exchange prayer requests. Invite them to share personal reflections on what the coming of God's promised "righteous branch from David's line" means to them (Jeremiah 33:15).

Sing or read aloud the hymn, "Come, Thou Long Expected Jesus." Close the session with the prayer for the First Sunday in Advent found in "How to Lead This Study" or one of your own.

---

*Unless otherwise indicated, source material for this session plan may be found in *The New Interpreter's Bible* and *The New Interpreter's Study Bible*.

2. Reflect the Messiah
BIBLE BACKGROUND

Malachi 3:1-4

Malachi is the concluding book of the prophets in the Jewish Bible and the last book of the entire Old Testament in the Christian Bible. It is likely that this short book, containing only fifty-five verses, was written during the post-exilic period, probably after the rebuilding of the Jerusalem Temple and its dedication in 516 or 515 B.C. Although this prophetic book does not soar to the poetic heights of Isaiah, there is much to be gleaned from it. Major covenant themes that earlier prophets addressed—justice, concern for the vulnerable widow, orphan, and worker—are found in Malachi. So too are concerns about the Temple and the priesthood, which were important institutions for the people of Judah in the post-exilic era. Also evident in this book is a description of the Day of the Lord and the messenger who will come before that day. Some scholars believe that verses 4-6 were a later addition to this book. Whether part of the original book or added later, the prophesy in Malachi 4:5-6 regarding Elijah as the prophet who would come before the Lord's day became especially important to early Christian understandings of John the Baptist. Matthew 11:10, Mark 1:2, Luke 1:76, and Luke 7:27 all draw a line from Elijah to John, indicating that John is the returned Elijah. The relationship between John the Baptist and Jesus was also of great concern to the early church. The first Christians immediately established a connection between Malachi 3:1-3 and the Messiah.

The focus on the four verses for today's lection is that of the purification of the priesthood, which had become corrupted. God will send a messenger to accomplish this task. This purification is compared to the refining of precious gold and silver until all the impurities have been removed. Although these verses in Malachi are well known because they are featured in Handel's *Messiah*, two other prophets, Jeremiah (9:7) and Zechariah (13:9) also compare purification to the refinement of metals.*

Philippians 1:3-11

After greeting his readers, Paul typically gave thanks for them. Here in verses 3-11 he reported on his prayers of thanksgiving for the members of the church at Philippi and for the friendship and financial support they offered to him. Having established the church in the major city of Macedonia, Paul maintained very close ties to this church. Philippians is one of Paul's letters from prison (1:7). The letter was likely written between A.D. 52 and A.D. 62, but since the place of his imprisonment cannot be established, scholars cannot agree on a definite date.

Paul's prayer in verses 3-11 is divided into two parts. In verses 3-8, he listed the reasons for his gratitude toward the Philippian congregation. In verses 9-11, he made several prayer requests. Joy (verse 4), which sets the tone for this letter, is referenced again in 1:18; 2:2, 17; 3:1; 4:1, 4, 10. Paul wanted the church at Philippi to know that he remained joyful and glad even while in prison. Moreover, he was hopeful about the outcome.

One of the reasons for Paul's joy, according to verses 3-8, is that the Philippians had shared much. Philippians 1:5 refers to them as being Paul's "partners in the ministry of the gospel." Just how the church members shared is not spelled out, though references to Euodia and Syntyche and other "coworkers" in 4:2-3 indicate that people from the Philippian congregation have worked closely with Paul. We do know that they shared as "partners in God's grace" (1:7), lived according to the gospel (1:27), and made contributions to support Paul in his ministry (4:16).

Paul's intercessory prayer in verses 9-11 was not for himself but for the Philippian church. He prayed that their love would increase and that they would grow deeper in their knowledge. Paul prayed for this greater insight so that believers would be ready for "the day of Christ" (verse 10), his second coming. Paul was eager for these church members to be pure and righteous so that they would "give glory and praise to God" (verse 11).*

Luke 3:1-6

These six verses set the stage for John the Baptist and his proclamation about the coming of Christ. Just as Luke recorded the political events surrounding Jesus' birth (2:1-2), so too Luke clarified the political and religious leadership that was in charge as John began his work of preparing people for Jesus. Naming rulers was the traditional way Greco-Roman historians used to establish a timeframe. Luke named five imperial rulers—Tiberius, Pontius Pilate, Herod, Philip, and Lysanias—plus the two high priests—Annas and Caiaphas—who were serving at the time John emerged (3:1-2). Despite all this information, no date can be firmly fixed due to variations in ancient calendars. However, A.D. 28 fits well with Luke's information.

In addition to placing John the Baptist within a historical context, Luke made clear that John's coming and specific ministry had been foretold. John was surely the prophet that Isaiah expected to come and "cry out" to prepare a highway for God (Isaiah 40:3-5, quoted in Luke 3:4-5). Earlier, Luke had recorded the story of John's birth to an elderly, childless couple. In Luke 1, particularly in Zechariah's prophecy about his son in verses 76-77, this child, who "will be called a prophet of the Most High" will "go before the Lord to prepare his way" (1:76). John's message was a simple but profound one: He was to tell people "how to be saved through the forgiveness of their sins" (verse 77). John proclaimed this message and baptized people who repented and asked God to forgive their sins (3:3). He thereby fulfilled the prophecies made about him even as he prepared his people to hear and receive Jesus.

John was not the Messiah, and he told the crowds so (verse 16). He knew the limits of his authority and work, but his life, teachings, and baptism all pointed toward the promised Messiah. Those who listened and responded to John's call would be ready to respond to the ministry of gracious reconciliation that Jesus offered.*

LEARNING MENU

To consider how Christians prepare for Advent.

Reflect on preparing for Christmas

Supplies: large sheet of paper, markers, Preparing the Way

Post one or more large sheets of paper around the room. Have markers available. Greet participants as they arrive and encourage each one to write two or more activities that he or she is doing during this Advent season to prepare for Christmas on the paper. Have participants walk around the room and review the activities. Ask the following questions: How do these activities help us to prepare for the coming of Jesus? Which of these activities helps us to prepare spiritually? Which helps us to prepare in more material ways? As you review this list and think about your own activities, do you think that you need to readjust the balance between your spiritual and material preparations? If so, how? Save these lists for possible use during the Christmas Eve session.

Choose a volunteer to read the introduction to "Reflect the Messiah" in *Preparing the Way.* Encourage participants to relax and reflect on each question as you read it aloud. Be sure to pause long enough so that the adults have time to respond silently. How would you like Christ to find you when he returns? What is missing in your life? What is just needless clutter in your life? What type of spiritual "housecleaning" might you be doing as you look toward his arrival? Invite volunteers to comment to the group on any insights or surprises they discovered as they thought about their own lives.

*To hear and understand the prophet's words about
being refined into righteousness
(Malachi 3:1-4).*

A Discuss Paul's argument concerning Abraham's faith

Supplies: Bibles, Preparing the Way

Use information from the Bible Background and the first two paragraphs of "Refining into Righteousness" in *Preparing the Way* to present a brief lecture that will set the stage to study the text. Choose a volunteer to read Malachi 3:1-4. Discuss these questions: How did God respond to the people's concern that God was not upholding the covenant? What do you know about the process of silver refinement? How might this process be an appropriate metaphor for the purification of the levitical priests (Malachi 3:3)? What connections did the early church make between these four verses from Malachi and John the Baptist? How has the church connected these verses with the life and ministry of Jesus? Although this Scripture lesson focuses on the refinement of the levitical priests, we too live in a world that needs to be purified. What changes would you expect to see in the church if believers were to become serious about seeking God's purification? What action can you take this week to reflect God's presence in our world?

B Read a story of the refiner's touch

Supplies: Bibles

Enlist a volunteer to read Malachi 3:1-4. Note that these verses have challenged many people who have studied them. Then read this story:

One member of a Bible study group decided to learn firsthand what the refining process entailed by going to visit a silversmith at work. The woman was surprised to learn that throughout the entire process the silversmith needed to sit near the hottest part of the fire—the part that could most effectively burn off the impurities. She also learned that the silversmith had to keep his eye on the piece the entire time, for silver will be destroyed if it is heated too long. After sitting in silence as she watched the silversmith work, she finally asked, "How do you know when the silver is fully refined?" Smiling at her, he answered, "Oh, that's the easy part—when I see my image reflected in it."[2]

Discuss the following questions: Had you been the woman who had gone to observe this process, what would you say to the other members of your study group about this process and how it relates to Malachi's words? Note that the refiner's image appears when the impurities have all been removed. What does this fact suggest about how we humans reflect the image of God and God's Messiah, who himself is "the imprint of God's being" (Hebrews 1:3)?

C Hear Malachi's words set to music

Supplies: Bibles, music of Handel's Messiah, appropriate music player

Read aloud Malachi 3:1-4 as expressively as possible. Point out that in the famous oratorio *Messiah*, the composer George Frideric Handel used Malachi 3:1 for section 5, the "Recitativo accompagnato"; Malachi 3:2 for section 6, "Air"; and Malachi 3:3 for section 7 for the "Chorus."[3] Play these three sections and then discuss these questions: How did this music animate the words? What new insights about this Scripture could you discern by listening to the music?

To explore Paul's description of a discerning faith
(Philippians 1:3-11).

A Discuss the Bible text

Supplies: Bibles, Preparing the Way

Set the context for today's reading by preparing in advance to retell the story found in Acts 16:6-40 of Paul's vision that called him to Macedonia, his trip there, the conversion of Lydia as a result of Paul's ministry, his encounter with the slave woman, and the experiences of Paul and Silas in the prison at Philippi. Make your presentation brief, but remember that an understanding of what happened when Paul was present in Philippi will make his letter more meaningful to the participants. Select a volunteer to read Philippians 1:3-11. Encourage participants to use their Bibles and information about this Scripture in *Preparing the Way* to answer these questions. Add information from the Bible Background as it seems appropriate. Based on today's reading, how would you describe Paul's general mood? How would you describe Paul's relationship with this congregation? Why is Paul grateful to this congregation? In verses 9-11, Paul offered a prayer for the congregation. What does Paul want for it?

B Discuss questions about faith

Supplies: Bibles, large sheets of paper, markers

Solicit a volunteer to read Philippians 1:3-11. Lead participants in reading verse 9 in unison. Have the group form teams of two or three. Give each team a large sheet of paper. Ask: What are some questions that you have about your faith as a follower of Christ? Have the teams list their questions on the large sheet of paper. Tell them to discuss possible responses to these questions. After a few moments, invite the teams to report highlights of their discussions to the entire group.

C Write an intercessory prayer for the church

Supplies: Bibles, paper, pencils

Invite a volunteer to read Philippians 1:3-11. Read aloud the final paragraph in the Bible Background for Philippians, which indicates reasons that Paul prayed for this congregation. Distribute paper and pencils. Encourage participants to reflect silently on reasons to pray for their congregation. Try to focus on petitions that will help the church members grow into a deeper relationship with Christ. Suggest that each participant write a prayer using two or three of the reasons he or she has identified. Challenge participants to pray their prayers each day in the coming week.

To meet John the Baptist, who has come out of the wilderness
(Luke 3:1-6).

A   Delve into the biblical text

Supplies: Bibles, Preparing the Way

Introduce today's Gospel passage by reading or reviewing highlights of information from the Bible Background. Choose someone to read Luke 3:1-6. Have participants review the section "Coming Out of the Wilderness" in *Preparing the Way*. Discuss these questions: What do you know about the political context in which John the Baptist ministered? What do you know about John from the biblical account and from reviewing "Coming Out of the Wilderness"? What does the fact that John came out of the wilderness suggest about him? In Luke 3:4-5 we find a quotation from Isaiah 40:3-5. What does Luke's use of this quotation suggest about how the early church viewed John the Baptist? What role does John the Baptist play in your own faith journey?

B   Encounter a prophecy

Supplies: Bibles, Preparing the Way

Invite a participant to read Isaiah 40:3-5 and then immediately read Luke 3:4-5 from the same translation. Suggest that the rest of the group listen carefully to compare the two passages. Discuss how Luke's version of Isaiah is similar to and different from the original (note that the location of the voice is different). To augment the discussion, select a volunteer to read the paragraph in *Preparing the Way* that begins "Luke 3:4-6 quotes Isaiah 40:3-5, which is a powerful vision." Ask these questions: Luke's original audience heard these words roughly 50 years after Jesus' death and resurrection. What does this suggest about the early church's thinking about John and his relationship to Isaiah's prophecy? How would you say that John fulfilled the prophecy as "a voice crying out"? What connection do you see between John's call to repent and change the orientation of one's life and the prophecy that "all humanity will see God's salvation" (verse 6)?

C   Imagine hearing and responding to John's call to repent

Supplies: Bibles

Select a volunteer to read Luke 3:1-6. Lead participants to respond to John's call by reading this guided imagery. Be sure to pause long enough to allow time for silent reflection. Suggest that participants relax in their chairs and close their eyes to envision the following scene you will read:

You are walking along the Jordan River when you notice that a crowd has gathered. You move closer and see a man dressed in camel's hair with a leather belt around his waist. You wonder who this is. Could this scruffy-looking man be the long-awaited prophet Elijah who was to herald the Messiah's coming? And if so, what does his presence mean? (pause)

You hear this man preaching fervently, calling those in the audience to repent and turn their lives around. You begin to think about areas in your own life where you know you fall short of God's expectations. Silently you talk with God about your sins and seek forgiveness. (pause)

Hear God say that you are forgiven. Let the peace of God fill you and give thanks. (pause)

Open your eyes when you are ready.

Invite participants to share any insights or inspirations they may have gained during this experience.

To go forth to reflect the Messiah.

Make a commitment to reflect Christ

Supplies: large sheet of paper, marker, mirror(s), hymnals

Thank the participants for coming today and suggest that they read Chapter 3 of *Preparing the Way* before the next session.

Read today's additional Scripture from Luke 1:68-79 responsively if your hymnal includes the "Canticle of Zechariah," also known as the "Benedictus." Alternatively, invite half of the group to read the even-numbered verses and half to read the odd-numbered ones from their Bibles.

Challenge participants to identify characteristics of Jesus that they can emulate. Could they, for example, teach others about God, support someone who is in the process of healing, feed the hungry, be present for the lonely, or model discipleship for others? List their ideas on a large sheet of paper. Provide a few moments for participants to choose one or two of these characteristics that they could imitate this week.

Pass around one or more small mirrors. Encourage participants to look at themselves in the mirror and envision seeing the face of Christ. Invite them to echo this sentence after you: "We commit ourselves to following Christ so that others may see him reflected in us."

Sing "Toda la Tierra" ("All Earth Is Waiting") or another hymn appropriate to the Advent season. Close the session with the prayer for the Second Sunday of Advent found in "How to Lead This Study" or one of your own.

---

*Unless otherwise indicated, source material for this session plan may be found in *The New Interpreter's Bible* and *The New Interpreter's Study Bible*.

3. Prepare for Peace

BIBLE BACKGROUND

Zephaniah 3:14-20

In Zephaniah 1:1, the prophet introduced himself as "Zephaniah, Cushi's son." Since "Cush" referred to Ethiopia or Nubia, scholars debate whether Zephaniah was of African descent. What is clear from verse 1 is that his lineage reaches back four generations to Hezekiah, who may have been the Judean king who reigned from 715–687 B.C. God called Zephaniah to speak during the reign of King Josiah (640–609 B.C.), a king known for his positive reforms. A contemporary of the prophets Nahum and Jeremiah, Zephaniah was the first prophet since Isaiah, approximately 70 years earlier during Hezekiah's reign, to speak to the people in Judah about their disobedience to God.

The focus of Zephaniah's prophecy is "the Day of the LORD." Zephaniah 1:2–3:8 centers on announcements of judgment made against both Judah and the nations. Zephaniah also offered a word of hope in 3:9-20, where he announced God's salvation and restoration for both the nations and Jerusalem. Notice that the stark images of judgment (for example, 1:2, 12-15) in contrast to the comforting images of restoration (3:14-15, 19-20).

Today's lection from Zephaniah 3:14-20 is a joyous song of victory. These verses constitute the ninth oracle in this book comprised of only 53 verses divided into three chapters. Verses 14-17, which call Jerusalem to rejoice, pronounce a blessing upon the people. Notice that in verse 14 the people are urged to rejoice, but the unnamed voice who issued this call also reported that God "will rejoice over you with singing" (verse 17). In these verses God is described as both "the king of Israel" (verse 15) and "a warrior bringing victory" (verse 17). Verses 19-20, which may have been added by a later editor, spotlight what God will do to restore the people. Observe those who are specifically identified: "the lame" and "the outcast." These people who have been living on the margins will be delivered and gathered. Moreover, they will experience a reversal of status and fortune: Their shame will be changed to praise, and they will become famous throughout the earth. Their possessions will be restored, and their future will be different from their past.*

Philippians 4:4-7

Paul closed his letter to the Philippian congregation with several exhortations. First, in keeping with his emphasis on joy, which we noted in the previous session, Paul called the people to "be glad" or, as the NRSV puts it, "Rejoice." Being joyful was an important aspect of Paul's life as a Christian disciple. This gladness or joy was to be found "in the Lord" (verse 4).

The second exhortation, in verse 5, concerns how Christians are to relate to others. Believers are to be known for their gentleness. The Greek word translated here as "gentleness" "denotes generosity toward others and is a characteristic of Christ himself." Notice that this generosity is not limited to one's friends or family but is to be extended to "all people." Verse 5 also points out "the Lord is near." Whether that statement is to be understood in terms of space (that is, geographic closeness) or in terms of time (that is, the Lord will soon return), the point is that God's people should be glad and rejoice because of the Lord's nearness.

The command in verse 6 not to "be anxious about anything" calls to mind Jesus' teaching in Matthew 6:25-34, where he told us not to worry and assured us that God would take care of those whose first priority was God's kingdom. Paul urged his readers to lift their needs to God in prayer. These "prayers and petitions" (verse 6) are to be offered with thanksgiving.

According to verse 7, we can trust God to act on our behalf. We therefore can enjoy God's peace, which is to be understood as a complete sense of well-being. Believers who enter into the mind of Christ and share his attitude (Philippians 2:5) invite the heart and mind of Jesus to dwell in them.*

Luke 3:7-18

In the last session, we met John the Baptist. This week, we overhear his preaching and responses to it. Luke 3:7-18 may be divided into three parts: verses 7-9 warn people about impending judgment; verses 10-14 call people to ethical reforms; and verses 15-17 announce the coming of the Messiah. Verse 18 summarizes John's ministry of "proclaiming good news to the people."

John began his proclamation with a stinging condemnation of his audience, calling them "children of snakes" (verse 7). If we think about snakes slithering to escape a fire, we can easily relate this image to the people who had come to John to be baptized so as to escape the coming judgment. John's message, like that of Old Testament prophets such as Isaiah, Amos, and Zephaniah, was a warning about "the day of the Lord." Many of John's listeners were descendants of Abraham, with whom God had made covenant. Despite their relationship with one who was dear to God's heart, the people would not be able to count on their familial connections. They needed to change their hearts and lives. Unless they did so and began to produce "good fruit" (verse 9), they would be called to account, judged, and found wanting.

With judgment so near, the people cried out to ask what they should do. John's response was specifically tailored for three groups of people: the crowds, tax collectors, and soldiers. John admonished the crowds to share whatever food and clothing they had. He called on the tax collectors, who were notorious for overcharging, to assess only what was due. John urged the soldiers not to "cheat or harass anyone" and to be satisfied with their wages (verse 14). Note that all of John's responses call for a change in lifestyle so that one is no longer greedy and focused on amassing possessions.

Although John's audience wondered if he were the long-awaited Messiah, he assured them that he was not. He told them they would recognize the Messiah, for he would baptize with fire and, as the judge, would separate the good wheat (those who repented) from the worthless chaff.*

LEARNING MENU

To prepare for the Messiah.

Reflect on life changes

Supplies: Preparing the Way, two large sheets of paper, and marker, paper, pencils

Choose a volunteer to read the introduction to "Prepare for Peace" in *Preparing the Way*. Invite participants to think of a major event in their own lives (perhaps marriage, the birth or adoption of a child, launching a career) that transformed them in some way. Discuss these questions either with the entire group or in small teams. If you choose to work in small teams, write these questions on a large sheet of paper prior to the session.

1. What did you do to prepare for this change?
2. What behavioral or attitudinal changes did you see in yourself after this event occurred?
3. Would you say that the way you perceived yourself changed dramatically? If so, how?
4. What advice could you give someone who was facing a similar change?
5. How would you compare the time and energy you spent preparing for the change you cited to the time and energy you spend preparing for the coming and coming again of Christ?

Allow a moment or two for silent reflection concerning how Christ has transformed them through these events.

Distribute paper and pencils. Encourage individuals to write a brief devotional reflection based on the insights they have gained about changes in their lives. Suggest that they use one of the following Scriptures as part of their devotional reflection:

Isaiah 7:14: Immanuel will be born
Luke 1:67-75: The coming of a savior from the house of David
Luke 3:4-5: Preparations for the arrival of a king
John 1:1-14: The Word is the light of the world

Invite volunteers to read what they have written. Recommend that participants continue to work at home on their devotional guides.

To explore how God calms people with love
(Zephaniah 3:14-20).

A   Delve into Zephaniah's message

Supplies: Bibles, Preparing the Way

Read or retell the Bible Background for Zephaniah to provide an overview. Select a volunteer to read Zephaniah 3:14-20. Choose someone to read from "Calmed With Love" from *Preparing the Way* beginning with "The Book of Zephaniah" through "had been radically altered" to explain the reasons for God's righteous anger.

Suggest that participants scan the rest of "Calmed With Love" in order to answer these questions, which you will discuss: Why should the people of Jerusalem, who have been judged and punished by God, begin to rejoice? What images of God are presented in verses 15-17? (Note that God is both king and a victorious warrior.) What did God promise to do for the people? What good news do you hear in these verses?

B Plan a project to demonstrate God's love

Supplies: Bibles, large sheet of paper, marker

Choose a volunteer to read Zephaniah 3:14-20.

Discuss these questions: What does this passage tell you about God's love? God loves all people, but in this passage, several groups are specifically mentioned. Who are they? (List ideas on a large sheet of paper. Here are possibilities: victims of war, the fearful, the oppressed, those who are dealing with a handicapping condition, the exiles.)

Encourage participants to identify at least one of these groups to whom they could show God's love. If possible, discern people within the community with whom participants could interact over the next two or three weeks.

During Advent, many groups plan to provide Christmas gifts for children whose parents are incarcerated or whose families cannot afford gifts. Consider planning a visit to a nursing home to sing carols and provide toiletries or other items residents might need. Determine what you can do, when it will be done, for whom, by whom, and using what resources.

C Create a breath prayer

Supplies: Bibles, paper, pencils

Select a volunteer to read Zephaniah 3:14-20.

Suggest that one way participants may experience the calming peace and forgiveness of God's love is to use a phrase of praise or petition known as a breath prayer. Invite each participant to create a six- to eight-syllable prayer that has personal meaning and addresses a need or concern. Here are some examples: *Jesus, grant me your peace; Holy Spirit, dispel my fears; Father, let me feel your love.*

Provide time for participants to mull over and jot down ideas. Several volunteers may be willing to share their prayers. Encourage participants to refine their prayers at home and offer them often, perhaps on a cue, such as a clock striking the hour or a phone ringing. They may pray silently, aloud, or as a chant. Suggest that they practice this ancient form of prayer as a way of praying without ceasing.

To discover God's antidotes to worry
(Philippians 4:4-7).

A   Explore Paul's teaching

Supplies: Bibles, Preparing the Way

Select a volunteer to read Philippians 4:4-7. Lead participants in a verse-by-verse discussion by using the Bible Background for Philippians. Discuss these questions and suggest that participants may want to check "Don't Worry" in *Preparing the Way* for possible responses. What benefit do you think Paul found in being glad or rejoicing in the Lord at all times? What did Paul mean when he urged his readers to let their gentleness show (verse 5)? In what ways was the Lord near to Paul, to his readers, and to you? How does prayer provide an antidote to anxiety and worry? Paul not only told people to bring their petitions to God but also to give thanks. Why do you think many believers find it easier to make requests than to offer thanks? How do you experience "the peace of God" (verse 7)? What changes might you expect to see in the church and wider community if Christians really took Paul's teachings seriously?

B   Write a journal entry

Supplies: Bibles, Preparing the Way, paper, pencils

Solicit a volunteer to read the section "Don't Worry" in *Preparing the Way* beginning with "'Don't worry'" and ending with "relied on God." Note that Paul had many reasons to be worried, but he remained calm by trusting in God. Call for a volunteer to read Philippians 4:4-7.

Distribute paper and pencils. Suggest that participants scan the remainder of "Don't Worry." Then they are to write a journal or diary entry in which they (a) state a problem that has been gnawing at them, (b) explain how they have been trying to handle the problem, (c) add strategies suggested by Paul that they could use to deal with this issue more effectively. Before participants begin to write, state that these entries are confidential.

Conclude this activity by inviting volunteers to comment on a strategy that Paul used as an antidote to worry that they find useful.

C   Compare two Scriptures about trusting in God

Supplies: Bibles, Preparing the Way

Choose a volunteer to read Philippians 4:4-7. Invite participants to scan "Don't Worry" in *Preparing the Way* to find answers to this question: How did Paul say that he—and we—can find peace? Note that the prophet Isaiah also wrote about a new day when peace and justice would prevail. At this time, the shoot that is to come "from the stump of Jesse" (11:1) will rule. As Christians, we understand that "shoot" to be Jesus, the Messiah. He will come to rule in peace.*

Select another volunteer to read today's additional lectionary Scripture from Isaiah 12:2-6 as participants follow along in their Bibles. Discuss these questions: What evidence of trust in and thanksgiving for the God who is "my salvation" (verse 2) do you find in this passage? What relationship do you see between the ideas expressed in Philippians 4 and those expressed in Isaiah 12?

To investigate John the Baptist's message and people's responses (Luke 3:7-18).

A   Hear and respond to the message of John the Baptist

Supplies: Bibles, Preparing the Way

Choose one volunteer to read the part of John the Baptist in Luke 3:7-18 and another to read the narration. Invite everyone to read verse 10. Ask two people to read in unison the part of the tax collectors in verse 12 and another two to read the part of the soldiers in verse 14.

Clarify John's meaning and the people's responses by asking the following questions. Use information from the Bible Background for this passage to add to the discussion. John's harsh words about judgment would likely not hold the attention of a modern crowd. Why might his listeners have stayed to hear his message and then respond to him? What seems to be the point of John's comments about Abraham? Even though John's words were harsh, the crowd responded by asking John what they were to do. He gave a general answer to the crowd and specific answers to the tax collectors and the soldiers. How would you summarize his concerns? Why do you think the people "wondered whether John might be the Messiah" (verse 15)? How did John differentiate himself from the Messiah? In verse 17, John continued the theme of judgment by stressing how the Messiah will judge. In verse 18, Luke reports that John was "proclaiming good news to the people." What good news do you hear? How would you respond?

B   Delve into the Scripture passage

Supplies: Bibles, Preparing the Way, large sheet of paper, marker

Choose a volunteer to read Luke 3:7-18. Form four teams and assign them portions of "What, Then, Should We Do?" in *Preparing the Way*. Team 1 will read "What defines someone" through "stones on the ground!" Team 2 will read "John's words should send" through "kingdom in the world." Team 3 will read "Understandably" through "Acts 2." Team 4 will read "In ancient times" through "Jesus Christ."

Post these questions, which you have written prior to the session, for the groups to discuss:

1. What do you learn about John himself?
2. What do you learn from his message?
3. What do you learn about God's expectations for believers?

Bring everyone together and invite speakers from each team to report highlights of their discussions.

C Proclaim good news

Supplies: Bibles

Select a volunteer to read Luke 3:7-18. Read verse 18 again and ask: What would good news sound like to people in our community, our nation, or the world? What does it mean for Christians to agree to be radically transformed by baptism? Point out that John's words to the crowds, the tax collectors, and the soldiers all concerned social justice. To accept Christ requires more than verbal assent. A new way of life that expresses love for God by loving one's neighbor is absolutely necessary.

Discuss how your congregation is currently proclaiming good news in both word and deed. Think about mission and outreach ministries that you support. Then consider new avenues for service that will let others hear the good news and invite them into the kingdom of God. Encourage participants to pray about supporting current ministries and starting new ones.

To accept the peace the Messiah offers.

Exchange signs of peace.

Thank participants for coming today and encourage them to read Chapter 4 of *Preparing the Way* in preparation for the next session.

Sing "In the Bleak Midwinter" (*UMH*, 221). Pray the prayer for the Third Sunday of Advent found in "How to Lead This Study."

Invite participants to stand in a circle, if possible, and exchange signs of peace. Begin by asking one person to turn to the right and say, "May the peace of God be with you." That person will answer, "And also with you." Then, that person will turn to the person on his or her right and say, "May the peace of God be with you." Continue until everyone has heard the blessing of God's peace announced.

Close with this benediction from 2 Thessalonians 3:16, 18: "May the Lord of peace himself give you peace always in every way. The Lord be with all of you. . . .The grace of our Lord Jesus Christ be with all of you."

4. Images of the Messiah

BIBLE BACKGROUND

Micah 5:2-5a

This brief portion of Micah's prophecy begins by focusing on a place: "Bethlehem of Ephrathah" (verse 2). Bethlehem was a small town several miles south of Jerusalem that was first mentioned in Genesis 35:19 as the burial place of Rachel, the wife of Jacob (Israel). Naomi's husband Elimelech was from Bethlehem (Ruth 1:1). Eventually, the widowed Naomi returned to Bethlehem from Moab with her widowed Moabite daughter-in-law Ruth (1:22). Naomi's kinsman Boaz married Ruth, and they became the parents of Obed, grandparents of Jesse, and great-grandparents of David (4:17). Thus the reference to "Bethlehem of Ephrathah" not only located the city on a map but also brought historic connections with Israel's great king David (1 Samuel 17:12; Luke 2:4) to the forefront.

The ruler referred to in Micah 5:2 who would come forth from Bethlehem was understood in the early church to be Jesus. When the magi inquired of King Herod's scribes and chief priests about the birthplace of the Messiah (Matthew 2:4-6), they quoted Micah 5:2, saying that according to the prophet, he would be born in Judah in the town of Bethlehem. Micah 5:4 describes the ruler as the shepherd of God's people, Israel. This description of the shepherd king more closely links the One who is to come with both God and David. Ezekiel 34:23 names this shepherd as David, whom God called from his work as a young shepherd to be anointed as Israel's king by the prophet Samuel. In 2 Samuel 7:16, God made a covenant with David in which God promised that David's "throne will be established forever." Micah 5:4 and Ezekiel 34:23 refer to the shepherd's care: He shall feed the flock and keep it secure.

Micah 5:5 refers to the shepherd king as "one of peace." Similarly, Ezekiel 34:25 states that God will make with the people "a covenant of peace." Since Micah's words were originally addressed to Israelites already in exile or soon to be exiled to Babylon, the idea of a ruler from Bethlehem who would care for them as a shepherd king who creates peace and security must have been comforting indeed.*

Hebrews 10:5-10

Although known as "the Letter to the Hebrews" since the second century and attributed to Paul, this book does not conform to the format of a letter, was not written by Paul according to most scholars, and may not have been written for an audience of Hebrew Christians.

Today's lectionary reading comes from a section of Hebrews (8:1–10:18) that discusses Christ's ministry as the high priest. Specifically, the issue in Hebrews 9:1–10:18 is Christ's sacrifice. After discussing the sacrifices that needed to be made "continually every year" (10:1) the writer goes on to explain Christ's one-time sacrifice and how it affects believers.

Hebrews 10:5-7 is a quotation from Psalm 40:6-8, which is part of a song of thanksgiving. In Hebrews, these words have been attributed to Christ when he came "into the world" in the flesh (verse 5). According to Psalm 40:6 (as quoted in Hebrews 10:5-6), Christ said that God was not interested in "a sacrifice or an offering... entirely burned offerings or a sin offering." What Christ described was exactly the kind of animal sacrifices that were made in the Temple as prescribed by the mosaic law (verse 8). Instead, Christ himself has come to do God's will. The meaning and purpose of the "scroll" (verse 7) is unclear, in part because the Hebrew itself is unclear, though it may refer to a heavenly book kept by God. The wording of Psalm 40:7 ends with "I'm inscribed in the written scroll." In Hebrews 10:7, the fact that Christ has come to do God's will is what is written about him in the scroll.

Verse 10 makes clear the impact of Christ's sacrifice: "We have been made holy by God's will." Our holiness has come as the result of "the offering of Jesus Christ's body once for all." Unlike the sacrifices of the priests, Christ only needed to make a one-time sacrifice.*

Luke 1:39-45

This passage focuses on the visit and conversation between Mary and Elizabeth. In Luke 1:5-25, Luke reported that the aging Elizabeth, who had been barren during her normal childbearing years, would bear a son who was to be named John. In verses 26-38, Luke told the story of the Annunciation, how a young, unmarried woman was told by an angel that she would bear God's son. To convince Mary that "nothing is impossible for God" (verse 37), the angel Gabriel told her that her relative Elizabeth was now six months pregnant.

In verse 39, the two unlikely mothers-to-be met at Elizabeth's home in a village of the Judean hill country. Mary "got up and hurried" (verse 39) to get there, possibly indicating her wonder and desire to see Elizabeth as soon as possible.

When Mary entered the home, Elizabeth's unborn son "leaped in her womb," and she herself "was filled with the Holy Spirit" (verse 41). Gabriel's words were fulfilled, for clearly John was "filled with the Holy Spirit even before his birth" (verse 15). Under the power of the Spirit, Elizabeth was able to speak four oracles from God. The text gives no indication that Elizabeth knew anything about Gabriel's visit to Mary. Consequently, the Spirit must have guided Elizabeth as she proclaimed the blessedness of Mary and her unborn child. As Elizabeth asked why she should be so honored to be visited by Mary, Elizabeth confessed that Mary's unborn child was "[her] Lord" (verse 43). The third word Elizabeth spoke concerned her baby leaping for joy. This word hinted that John was already beginning to fulfill his purpose as the one who would help others to prepare for the coming of the Messiah. Finally, in verse 45 Elizabeth pronounced a beatitude on Mary. God had promised Mary that she would become the mother of God's Son (verse 35). Mary had believed God and that amazing promise was being fulfilled. Divine promises made to Zechariah and Elizabeth, as well as to Mary, are coming to fruition. Their stories become intertwined in the larger story of God's plan for salvation.*

LEARNING MENU

To introduce images of Jesus.

Consider images of Jesus

Supplies: pictures of Jesus, Preparing the Way, large sheet of paper, marker

Spread on a table or pass around pictures you have been able to locate of Jesus. You may find these in books or in Sunday school curriculum. Provide an opportunity for participants to see as many of these as possible. If time permits, take the group on a walking tour of the church to see pictures, stained glass windows, wall hangings, or other visual art that depicts Jesus. Discuss reasons why participants find some of these images endearing and others, perhaps, difficult to identify with or understand. Leave these pictures where they will be visible throughout the session, if possible.

Choose a volunteer to read the introduction to "Images of the Messiah" in *Preparing the Way*. Go around the room and invite each participant to name one image of Jesus. List these ideas on a large sheet of paper. More than one participant may give the same response but try for variety. Here are several possibilities among many: Savior, King, Prophet, Priest, Lamb of God, Babe in Bethlehem's manger, Crucified One, Prince of Peace, Healer, Teacher, Rabbi, and Shepherd. Form pairs and ask each person to select one or two images that have special meaning. Each person is to explain to his or her partner why this image is so appealing. Invite them to tell the entire group about their conversations.

To explore the image of Jesus as shepherd
(Micah 5:2-5a).

A   Hear a prophecy about a shepherd king

Supplies: Bibles, Preparing the Way

Choose a volunteer to read Micah 5:2-5a. Encourage participants to review "The Shepherd" in *Preparing the Way*. Discuss the following questions. Include information from the Bible Background to fill in gaps. What associations would Bethlehem of Ephrathah bring to mind for those who heard Micah's prophecy? What information does the prophet provide about the ruler who is to come? How might Micah's words have been received by Israelites who heard them at the time when the Northern Kingdom (Israel) was collapsing at the hands of the Assyrians in 721 B.C.? Christians have long interpreted this passage as a prophecy about Jesus. How do you see him fulfilling this prophecy?*

B Study biblical references to shepherds

Supplies: Bibles, Bible concordances, papers, pencils

Select a volunteer to read Micah 5:2-5a. Form several small teams and give each one a concordance. Assign each group specific books of the Bible to find the word "shepherd" in their concordance and see how it is used. The word "shepherd(s)" is found in the following books: Genesis, Numbers, 2 Samuel, 1 Kings, 1 Chronicles, 2 Chronicles, Psalms, Ecclesiastes, Isaiah, Jeremiah, Ezekiel, Amos, Micah, Zechariah, Matthew, Mark, John, Acts, Hebrews, 1 Peter, and Revelation.[4] Have the teams discuss these questions: What positive attributes did you find concerning shepherds? What negative attributes did you discover? To whom were these negative characteristics attributed? Often the Bible refers to God as the shepherd of the people. Which examples from your assigned books used "shepherd" in reference to God? What did you learn about God from these passages? Do you agree that the image of a shepherd is a fitting image for Jesus? Why or why not?

C Locate hymns about shepherds

Supplies: Bibles, hymnals, paper, pencils, large sheet of paper, marker

Choose a volunteer to read Micah 5:2-5a. Note particularly verse 4, where this ruler of Israel, who is to come from Bethlehem, is described as a shepherd. Distribute hymnals, paper, and pencils to each participant. Prior to the session, check the hymnals you use for these titles and write ones included in the hymnal on a large sheet of paper: "Savior, Like a Shepherd Lead Us"[5]; "The Lord's My Shepherd, I'll Not Want"[6]; "The King of Love My Shepherd Is"[7]; "O Thou, in Whose Presence"[8]; "You Satisfy the Hungry Heart"[9]; and "Shepherd Me, O God."[10] Encourage participants to select at least one of the hymns and read it carefully. Discuss these questions: What qualities does the hymn writer highlight in the shepherd? What actions, if any, does the shepherd take in this hymn? What attracts you toward, or repels you from, this portrayal of the shepherd? Would you say that this hymn accurately reflects the biblical descriptions you know of the Good Shepherd? Explain your answer. Invite teams to share highlights of their discussions. Reassemble as one group and sing one or more verses of selected hymns as time permits.

To understand the image of Jesus as sacrificial priest
(Hebrews 10:5-10).

A   Discuss the role of the priest

Supplies: Bibles, Preparing the Way

Select a volunteer to read Hebrews 10:5-10. Provide time for participants to review "The Sacrificial Priest" in *Preparing the Way*. Discuss these questions together: What were the qualifications and functions of the high priest? Why did the people believe that it was necessary to cleanse the Temple each year? According to the writer of Hebrews, the sacrificial system was flawed. Why? How did the incarnate Jesus change the relationship between the people and God? Jesus' sacrifice eliminated the need for ritual sacrifices, but we still need to repent of our sins. Why? What does the image of Jesus as the high priest who offers himself as the ultimate sacrifice suggest to you about giving yourself to others?

B   Discern the message of Hebrews 10 in relation to the contemporary church

Supplies: Bibles, Preparing the Way

Choose a volunteer to read Hebrews 10:5-10. Read these selected passages from "The Sacrificial Priest" in *Preparing the Way*: "Hebrews 10:5-10 contrasts the role of Jesus as high priest against the ancient understanding of high priests and the ritual practice of sacrifice. . . . According to the writer of Hebrews, the system is flawed. Psalm 40:6-8, rephrased in Hebrews 10:5-7, says that what God really wants is not empty ritual but people who do God's will and have God's law within them. These words echo the ancient prophetic warnings against excessive dependence on ritual and their call to obey God's will and observe God's law within the heart. Hebrews 10:7 interprets Psalm 40:6-8 with the voice of Jesus who says, 'Look, I've come to do your will, God.' "

Discuss these questions: According to Hebrews 10, God does not want empty rituals but obedient people. Do you think rituals in the church are empty? Why or why not? How does Jesus as the high priest serve as an example of one who does the will of God? What lessons can we learn from Jesus about obedience? About self-giving?

C   Paraphrase the main points

Supplies: Bibles, Preparing the Way

Solicit a volunteer to read Hebrews 10:5-10. Participants may wish to review "The Sacrificial Priest" in *Preparing the Way*. Invite participants to state in their own words the main points of this passage. Ask: How do these points help you to better understand the image of Jesus as the high priest?

To recognize the unborn Jesus as the child of promise
(Luke 1:39-45).

A   Overhear the conversation between Mary and Elizabeth

Supplies: Bibles, Preparing the Way

Set the stage for today's Gospel lesson by reading or retelling information from the Bible Background for Luke 1. Read Luke 1:39-45 as a drama by enlisting one volunteer to read the part of Elizabeth and another to read the narration. (Note that Mary does not speak.) Learn more about this encounter between these two pregnant women by encouraging participants to review silently "A Child in the Womb" in *Preparing the Way*. Discuss the following questions: Suppose you had been a neighbor of Mary's family. What would you have thought about this young, unmarried girl being pregnant? How would you have treated her? Suppose you had gossiped about Elizabeth's childless state, perhaps making snide remarks through the years about God's apparent disfavor of her. What would you be saying *about* her now that she has become pregnant past normal childbearing years? What would you be saying *to* her? When Elizabeth and Mary meet, the unborn John responded by leaping in the womb. What might that suggest about John and his future relationship with Jesus? How did the Spirit-filled Elizabeth respond to Mary? How might Elizabeth's statements to Mary in verses 42-45 help you to celebrate the birth of Jesus Christ?

B   Roleplay a conversation between Mary and Elizabeth

Supplies: Bibles

Choose a volunteer to read Luke 1:39-45. Select two participants to roleplay more of the conversation that could have occurred between Mary and Elizabeth. Here are several topics for discussion: (a) how each woman felt about being a mother under unusual circumstances; (b) what each woman thought she knew about the child she was carrying; (c) how each woman felt that God was working in her own life; (d) what each woman believed that her husband thought about this pregnancy and the child who was to be born. (If time permits, more than one team may do the roleplay.) Debrief this roleplay with the rest of the participants by asking: Had you been present for this conversation, what questions would you have asked Elizabeth or Mary? Encourage participants to suggest possible answers.

C Analyze Mary's response to Elizabeth

Supplies: Bibles, optional hymnals

Read today's lection from Luke 1:39-45. Note that Elizabeth's words end with a beatitude, a word of blessing, on Mary who has believed God's promises. Point out that although today's lectionary reading ends here, the additional reading for this Fourth Sunday in Advent follows immediately in Luke 1:46b-55. Choose a volunteer to read this passage, known as Mary's "Magnificat," or distribute hymnals that include this passage and invite all participants to read responsively. Discuss these questions: Although people around Mary would likely ostracize and shame her for her apparent infidelity, how does she respond to her pregnancy? What does Mary believe about the nature of God? (Note that God is holy, merciful, strong, able to aid, and a promise-keeper.) What does Mary say that God has done? (Point out that God has basically turned the world upside down by reversing the expected order of relationships.) How does Mary characterize God's relationship with the Jewish people?

To celebrate distinct images of the Messiah.

Give thanks for the coming of the Messiah

Supplies: three large sheets of paper, marker

Thank the adults for their participation. Encourage them to read Chapter 5 in *Preparing the Way* prior to the final session.

Post three sheets of paper. Label them "Shepherd," "High Priest," and "Unborn Child of Promise," respectively. Invite participants to think about these images of the Messiah they have encountered today by asking the following questions. Record their ideas on the appropriate paper. What biblical associations does the image of shepherd have for you? How is the image of the Messiah as a shepherd a positive (or negative) image for you? What is your understanding of the role of the high priest? How does Jesus fulfill this role? Even in the womb, John the Baptist recognized Jesus and leaped for joy. How do you respond to the incarnation—Jesus coming in the flesh? Which of these three images is most significant for you? Why? (Note that participants may want to add other images that are meaningful to them, but try to keep the focus on the three we have explored today.)

---

*Unless otherwise indicated, source material for this session plan may be found in *The New Interpreter's Bible* and *The New Interpreter's Study Bible*.

5. Welcome the Messiah

Bible Background

Isaiah 9:2-7

From the early days of the Christian movement, Jesus was understood to fulfill the descriptions of the ideal king found in Isaiah 9. Although we would have expected the New Testament writers to quote this passage, only Matthew quoted Isaiah 9:1-2 (Matthew 4:15-16). Names that we routinely associate with Jesus—"Wonderful Counselor, Mighty God, Eternal Father, Prince of Peace" (verse 6)—appear nowhere in the New Testament. The focus on David's throne and his kingdom (verse 7) is apparent in the New Testament. Similarly, this king's "justice and righteousness" (verse 7) are hallmarks of Christian understanding of Jesus, but verse 7 is quoted nowhere in the New Testament. Yet, we know these verses, in part, because they are read on Christmas Eve in lectionary years A, B, and C.[11] This passage from Isaiah 9 is also well known because it is featured in Handel's *Messiah*.[12]

Isaiah 9:1-7 may have been written for the coronation of a king, possibly Hezekiah, when he ascended to the throne in 727 B.C. Isaiah predicted that lands conquered during the Syro-Ephraimitic war by Assyrian king Tiglath-Pileser in 733–732 B.C. would be recovered, paving the way for the unification of the Northern and Southern Kingdoms.[13] More likely, these verses were written sometime after 732 B.C. to herald the birth of a descendant of David who would deliver the people. This date accords well with the events that occurred right after the Syro-Ephraimitic war of 734 B.C. At that time the people would be looking for a righteous king to lead them.

Isaiah 9:2-7 is a hymn of thanksgiving divided into two parts. The trouble that the people have experienced and their salvation are described in verses 2-3. In the second part, three reasons for giving thanks are listed, each beginning with the word "for" in the NRSV (verses 4, 5, 6). Note the use of "you" in the beginning of this hymn. These words are addressed to God.*

Titus 2:11-14

These four verses summarize the good news. Verses 11 and 13 hold in tension the time between Jesus' incarnation to bring "salvation to all people" and "the glorious appearance" when he comes again. As we have seen throughout Advent, we look back to celebrate the birth of the child in a manger, and we look ahead with hope to welcome the glorified savior, Jesus Christ.

As we live in the time between these two transformational events, questions arise such as, What shall we do? How shall we live? Titus 2:1-10 provided information as to how believers were to live in community within several relationships: husbands and wives, parents and children, masters and slaves. These household codes provided guidelines for Christian living within the parameters of the first century Roman society. While the rules for godly living presented in these verses are likely jarring to contemporary Christians, they did provide broader boundaries within these relationships than were customarily seen at the time. Creating a credible Christian witness was a strong motivation for believers to live in accordance with these codes.

The writer goes on to explain in verse 12 that God's grace provides believers with what they need to know in order to live a godly life. God's grace "educates us," thereby molding our characters so that we may choose to live "sensible, ethical, godly lives." Just as God's grace enables believers to make positive choices, they may reject "ungodly lives and the desires of this world" (verse 12).

In verse 13, the writer refers to "Jesus Christ" not only as "savior" but also more fully as "our great God and savior." This description clearly indicates that God becomes known to humans, insofar as is possible, through Christ. Moreover, this is only one of several instances where Christ is referred to as God (see John 1:1, 18; 20:28; Hebrews 1:8; possibly Romans 9:5). Verse 14 reports that Christ "gave himself for us" to "rescue" and "cleanse" believers so that they will be "eager to do good actions."*

Luke 2:1-20

In contrast to the detailed accounts of Gabriel's appearances to Zechariah and Mary, the story of Mary meeting Elizabeth at her home, and the birth and naming of John, the story of Jesus' birth is told with few details. Verses 1-5 set the political stage, explaining why Joseph and Mary had to leave their home in Nazareth and travel to Joseph's hometown of Bethlehem to participate in a census ordered by Caesar Augustus. While difficulties emerge with the historical evidence for the census, the section serves to place the birth within the political context of the day and to point to Jesus as the bringer of peace rather than Caesar Augustus. This child who was to bring peace was expected to be born in David's city. Somehow, Joseph and Mary had to get from Nazareth to Bethlehem. This census, purportedly ordered by an emperor responsible for great oppression, provided a plausible reason for the soon-to-be parents to make such a trek, particularly so late in Mary's pregnancy.

Verses 6-7 simply report that Mary birthed her son, snugly wrapped him in bands of cloth (as was the custom of the day), and placed him in a feeding trough because there were no proper accommodations available for them. These two verses emphasize the humility of the birth of the Savior and foreshadow his future. Just as there was no room in an inn or guest room in a home, many people would not open their hearts to Jesus.

In keeping with the humbleness of Jesus' birth, it is to lowly shepherds that the angel of the Lord announced the "wonderful, joyous news for all people" of this momentous event (verse 10). And this is the news: a savior, "Christ the Lord," has just been born in David's city (verse 11). Revelation prompts response, and so the shepherds traveled to Bethlehem, and after finding the holy family, reported what the angel had said to them. After telling their story to an amazed audience, the shepherds returned home, "glorifying and praising God" (verse 20). Their experience confirmed everything that they had been told.

LEARNING MENU

To welcome the Messiah on Christmas Eve.

Discern ways in which Christ's coming affects the world

Supplies: Preparing the Way, large sheets of paper saved from the opening of the second session, large sheets of paper with discussion questions

Solicit a volunteer to read the introduction to "Welcome the Messiah" found in *Preparing the Way*. Discuss these questions: Where do you see evidence that the earth is being transformed into God's kingdom? What is your vision for Christ's redeemed world? How will that new world be different from the one we know? What can you do right now to help usher in this kingdom where all will be healed and redeemed? Given your expectations for this kingdom, what can you do within the next twenty-four hours to welcome Christ and to share news of his arrival with others?

Encourage participants to name ways that they have prepared for Christmas. (If you have saved the list created during the opening of the second session, post that information again now.) Form small teams and invite participants to comment on any disparities between their intentions to prepare for Christ's arrival and what they actually accomplished. Prior to the session, write the following questions on a markerboard:

1. As you have thought about priorities for preparation throughout this season, which activities seem most important to you?
2. Were these the activities that you focused on? Why or why not?
3. How would you rate the balance between your spiritual preparations and material preparations, such as buying gifts and decorating your home?
4. If there were shortfalls in your spiritual preparations, how do you think these deficiencies have affected your ability to welcome the Messiah?
5. Based on this evaluation, what changes do you hope to make next year? Tell the teams to discuss responses to them. Have them share highlights of their discussions with the reassembled group.

To interpret the Messiah's coming in light of Isaiah's prophecy
(Isaiah 9:2-7).

A Study Isaiah's prophecy

Supplies: Bibles, Preparing the Way

Call for a volunteer to read Isaiah 9:2-7. Solicit readers for "He Will Be Named..." in *Preparing the Way*. Ask each volunteer to read at least one paragraph. Discuss these questions. Familiarize yourself with the Bible

Background for Isaiah 9 prior to the session so that you can add information to the conversation, as it seems appropriate. How did the Assyrians create a crisis for Judah? What do the "throne names" listed in verse 6 tell you about the One who will occupy David's throne? What else do you learn from this passage about the rule of this One who is to come? Had you been one of Isaiah's original hearers, how might this prophecy have affected you? How might our world be similar to the world of Isaiah and the world of first century Palestine into which Jesus was born? Based on Isaiah's prophecy, what reasons do you have to be eager to welcome this Messiah?

B Discover messianic prophecies of Jesus' coming in Isaiah

Supplies: Bibles, large sheet of paper, marker, optional commentaries

Invite a volunteer to read Isaiah 9:2-7. Read or retell the Bible Background for Isaiah. Point out that Isaiah includes many prophecies that, centuries later, Christians came to understand as references to Jesus. List on large paper the following selected prophecies from Isaiah: 7:14; 9:6-7; 11:1-5; 11:10; 16:5. Have the participants form teams of two or three. Tell the teams to look up the Scriptures and discuss what ideas Christians later gleaned from these words. Ask: What do they offer that help us to understand Jesus? Set out commentaries if you choose to have participants use them. Invite each team to tell the entire group about the highlights of their discussion.

C Celebrate the Messiah's arrival

Supplies: Bibles, hymnals, paper, pencils, large sheet of paper, marker

Select a volunteer to read Isaiah 9:2-7.
Distribute hymnals that you regularly use. If possible, also distribute copies of other hymnals or Christmas carol collections. Form several small teams. Invite team members to look through their music books to find descriptions of Jesus and his kingdom. Tell participants to jot down the title, page number, and descriptive phrases that they find.
Bring everyone together. Call on the teams in turn to name one hymn and the descriptions they found there. List these ideas on a large sheet of paper or markerboard. Ask: Which of these words or phrases best describe the Messiah for whom you have waited during this Advent? Are there any descriptive words that you would want to question the composer about? If so, what problems do you see with his or her interpretation? Which songs contain descriptions that are similar to the ones found in Isaiah 9? Of the songs that you have heard about today (or know from other sources), which one prompts you to celebrate Jesus' birth most joyously? Why?

To discern how to live in Christ
(Titus 2:11-14).

A   Explore the message to Titus

Supplies: Bibles, Preparing the Way

Choose several volunteers to read Titus 2:11-14, each from a different translation. Hearing different words will help participants to discover nuances in this passage. Read these words from *Preparing the Way*: "One of the common criticisms of Christians is that they do not behave differently than anyone else. Christians can be just as thoughtless, cruel, and mean as other people. These may be the same people who go to church every week, study their bibles daily, and profess a strong faith.... Those who live and work with us may see little evidence of our faith." Discuss these questions: We are recipients of God's grace, which has brought us salvation. How does grace help us to live the way that Jesus wants us to live? What criteria do you use to determine what is "sensible, ethical, and godly" versus what is "ungodly" (verse 12)? Give specific examples, if possible. What did Jesus' appearance on earth accomplish on our behalf? What expectations do you think Jesus has for our behavior?

B   Respond to a case study

Supplies: Bibles

Choose a volunteer to read Titus 2:11-14. Read this case study and invite participants to comment on ways that the situation can be resolved in a grace-filled manner.

Landon and Lucille raised their son Jeremy to follow biblical teachings. Jeremy has had the benefit of loving parents who regularly brought him to church and Sunday school with them. These parents thought they had set a godly example, and so were shocked to find that sixteen-year-old Jeremy had become sexually active and would soon be a father. Before meeting with the mother-to-be and her parents, Landon and Lucille sit down to talk with Jeremy. What can they say to begin the process of helping him to accept responsibility for his actions and also experience God's grace? How do you think God's grace is present for these families?

C   Describe God's grace

Supplies: Bibles, paper, pencils

Select a volunteer to read Titus 2:11-14. Read verse 11 again. Ask: How do you define "grace"? (A standard definition is "the free and unmerited act through which God restores his estranged creatures to himself."[14])

What does God's grace accomplish, according to this verse? Read 2 Timothy 1:9-10. How are these verses similar in meaning to the verses in Titus? Distribute paper and pencils. Invite participants to draw a circle in the center of their papers with spokes radiating from the circle to look like a bicycle wheel. Have them write the word "grace" in the center of the circle. On the spokes, they are to write words or phrases that describe what grace means to them, possibly including ideas from their discussion. Provide time for participants to share what they have written. Which words or phrases are repeated most often? Conclude by asking, How does God's grace enable us to live each day until Christ comes again?

To investigate Luke's account of Jesus' birth
(Luke 2:1-20).

A Appreciate the wonder of Jesus' birth

Supplies: Bibles, Preparing the Way

Read Luke 2:1-20 yourself, or prior to the session arrange for an expressive reader to be prepared to read. Encourage participants to close their eyes as the Scripture is read and try to hear this story for the first time. Form several small teams. Read these questions and allow time for participants to respond within their groups. Why might Luke have been so careful about setting the political scene? Why might Luke have told the actual birth story so sparingly with so few details? In contrast to the wealthy and powerful magi who appear in Matthew's account, shepherds are the first ones to hear the good news in Luke's story. They are also the first to tell others what they have witnessed. How do you think the news of Jesus' birth would have been received from these untutored laborers living on the fringes on society? Verse 19 reports, "Mary committed these things to memory and considered them carefully." Given what Mary already knew from Gabriel's announcement (1:26-38), the unborn John's reaction (1:41), and Elizabeth's response (1:42-45), what do you think Mary may have been pondering about the son she had just delivered? Did today's reading spark any new insights or raise any new questions? If so, what were they? Even if you have heard this story for decades, what about it evokes wonder in you?

B Explore Luke's understanding of the Christ

Supplies: Bibles, Preparing the Way

Choose a volunteer to read Luke 2:1-7, another to read verses 8-9, a third for verses 10-14, and a fourth for verses 15-20. Ask: What does this passage tell us about who Jesus is and what he will do? After some ideas are presented, suggest that participants scan "God With Us" in *Preparing the*

Way to see what other ideas they can add. In what ways do you see Jesus fulfilling Luke's understanding of him?

C   Make a commitment to spread the good news

Supplies: Bibles, large sheet of paper, marker, paper, pencils

Read Luke 2:1-20 as a drama. Select a narrator, one person for verses 10-12, and ask the entire group to read verse 14 in whichever translations they have. Ask: How did the shepherds respond to the angels' amazing news? How might the shepherds' response to the angels' message be a model for us? List ideas on the large sheet of paper.

Distribute paper and pencils. Encourage participants to make a commitment to follow the shepherds' example by spreading the good news of the Savior's birth. Invite them to write down one way they can spread the good news with their actions or their words in the week ahead. Tell them to keep their written commitments with them during the week as a reminder.

To bring the Advent journey to a close.

Review the Advent journey

Supplies: Preparing the Way, paper, pencils, hymnals

Invite participants to skim through *Preparing the Way* to recall the sessions and what they have gleaned from them. Then ask: What ideas or stories were most helpful to you during this Advent season? Why? What surprised or troubled you as you studied these lectionary readings? Distribute paper and pencils. Challenge participants to write several sentences that summarize what they have gleaned from this study and how that knowledge will help them as they continue their spiritual journeys. State that what they write will be confidential, so they may be very specific.

Read Psalm 96, which is this week's additional Scripture reading. If your hymnal includes a Psalter, ask half of the participants to read the regular type and the other half to read the boldface type. Consider using a sung response if one is suggested for Christmas. If you do not have access to a Psalter, solicit one volunteer for Psalm 96:1-6, a second for verses 7-9, and a third for verses 10-13.

Read the prayer for Christmas Eve in "How to Lead This Study." Sing "Angels We Have Heard on High" or "Joy to the World" to conclude this study.

Thank all who have come for their participation and wish them a blessed Christmas.

[1]From Baptismal Covenant II, *The United Methodist Hymnal*, 42. I chose the last sentence, which is used for each prayer as a means of creating continuity through the season, because it emphasizes the Trinitarian nature of God.

[2]From *http://www.clarion-call.org/extras/malachi.htm*.

[3]From Handel's *Messiah* program from The Baltimore Symphony Orchestra.

[4]From *The NRSV Concordance Unabridged*, by John R. Kohlenberger, III (Zondervan, 1991).

[5] From *The United Methodist Hymnal*, 381.

[6] From *The United Methodist Hymnal*, 136.

[7] From *The United Methodist Hymnal*, 138.

[8] From *The United Methodist Hymnal*, 518.

[9] From *The United Methodist Hymnal*, 629.

[10]From *The Faith We Sing* (Copyright © 2000 by Abingdon Press); 2058.

[11]From *The United Methodist Book of Worship*, Lectionary Years A, B, C (Copyright © 1992 by The United Methodist Publishing House); page 228.

[12]From *http://www.worshipmap.com/lyrics/messiahtext.html* (11) "The people that walked in darkness"; Isaiah 9:2 (Matthew 4:16—website shows 3:16, which is wrong); "For unto Us a Child is born"; Isaiah 9:6.

[13] From *Eerdmans Dictionary of the Bible*, "Tiglath-Pileser", edited by David Noel Freedman (William B. Eerdmans Publishing Company, 2000); pages 1308-1309.

[14] From *A Handbook of Theological Terms*, by Van A. Harvey (Collier Books, Macmillan Publishing Company, 1964); page 108.

*Unless otherwise indicated, source material for this session plan may be found in *The New Interpreter's Bible* and *The New Interpreter's Study Bible*.

CPSIA information can be obtained at www.ICGtesting.com
Printed in the USA
LVOW080822111112

306699LV00002B/2/P